MAKING MONEY OUT OF DATA

The art and science of Analytics

SHAILENDRA KUMAR

MAKING MONEY OUT OF DATA
The art and science of Analytics

ABOUT THE STORIES IN THE BOOK
Although the stories in the book reflect real-life business success
stories, some names and identifying details have been changed to
protect the privacy of the people involved.

ISBN-13:978-1547021741
ISBN-10:1547021748

Cover art by Artist
Edited by Paul Ryan
Interior design by Shailendra Kumar

http://www.cognitivetoday.com/

Provide feedback on the book at:
email: shailend.kumar@gmail.com

Twitter: @meisShaily

First Edition

Printed in the U.S.A

Dedication
To my dear wife Shweta

Acclaim for
MAKING MONEY OUT OF DATA

"The world of data and analytics can be quite intimidating. It has scale, complexity, is changing rapidly and is being both disrupted and enabled by massive technological change on a number of fronts. Business leaders cannot afford not to be investing in the space, but a key question is: where to start, without feeling as though you are trying to boil the ocean to eat a fish? Shailendra Kumar operates at the intersection between big data, technology and business fundamentals, and has that rare ability to take all of this complexity and break it down into very simple questions - about how can this improve our business? Through this ability, Shailendra helps business leaders better understand their customers, employees and competitors, and deliver insights that lead to improved business outcomes."

– Craig Dower, CEO, Salmat

"I have known Shailendra for over 10 years, observing his passionate commitment in educating others of the true power of Data Analytics. This book is the culmination of this passion and demonstrates how the true value of analytics can be realised. In this book, Shailendra explores what analytics really involves as opposed to what is commonly understood. He then shows how, by harnessing the power of data analysis, creative and innovative solutions can be found in order to drive extraordinary results. He does this with easy to understand case studies and how Advanced Data Analysis techniques were applied. Let Shailendra take you on a journey of how to gain the most of your data and maximize the potential you already have but are currently underutilizing."

– Maureen Thompson, Visit My Cat

"Making Money out of Data fulfills a longstanding void in content on analytics. One set of existing books focus on philosophy or survey of leading & lagging companies and correlate their success and sluggishness with application and absence of analytics. The other set of books/content is about the nitty gritty. Shailendra has addressed all key strategic question without acting as high priest of analytics and also addressed operational aspects without writing another 'analytics for dummies'. I have known Shailendra for over a decade and I noticed that he has extracted his deep and wide ranging experience in writing this book. He has been direct enough to bust popular myths at the same time humble enough to not call these myth busters as commandments of analytics. A reader would realize that these myth busters are actually key commandments which we all should follow as guide post while practicing analytics. The book goes a step further, it demonstrates what analytics can deliver and also delineates limitations. To me, this is the first attempt, at this scale, to de-mystify analytics and bring out its real value. I am sure, very soon, this would be a 'must read' for everyone who is keen to make it big through analytics."

– Sanjay Sharma, Managing Director, Accenture

"This book is a key primer for anyone who wants to lift the veil of mystique and hype around analytics. It makes things real. It makes them accessible. It supports it with war stories that relate the myths to results. Most importantly it is written by a passionate practitioner, who has seen the evolution of this discipline over the last couple of decades. Shailendra has got the stories, scars and suggestions, on what it takes to make analytics real, what it takes to move an idea to an applied business solution. He has an un-ending enthusiasm for the subject matter and absolute commitment to rise to the challenge, whether it is an applied one or one to educate the broader community about his passion – analytics."

– Marek Rucinski, Managing Director, Accenture

"Shailendra Kumar is an Analytics guru. In 'Making Money from Data' he brings to the forefront numerous examples of how to extract the most value from your #1 business asset; your customer data. He has a real talent for telling stories from the insights that were generated and the actions that were taken from his data analytics projects. Shailendra provides us with a fantastic insight into the world of using data analytics to drive revenue, increase profit whilst delivering a quality customer experience. This is a must read for any executive or business owner who is looking for an edge in using data (big and small) to drive a profitable outcome."

– Will Scully-Power, CEO of PASCAL51

"Making Money Out of Data" by Shailendra Kumar puts him head and shoulders above the crowd as a one in a billion thought leader and expert 'hands on' practitioner in Business & Data Analytics. Shailendra clearly has the ability to perform Jedi mind tricks with Data & Analytics, as clearly spelled out in 'Making Money Out Of Data' which illustrates a deeply compelling collection of proven examples of how to gain real and immediate value from your Data. This is a 'must read' guide for every business and technology decision maker, as well as anyone looking to learn more about the role Data now plays in our brave new world of 'data driven decisions'.

Shailendra conveys the core messages of this wonderful book in the form of five beautifully presented unique and engaging real world stories, ranging from the Olympic Games, Financial Services, Insurance, Retail, through to Federal Government digital technology initiatives.

– Dez Blanchfield, Founder & CEO - GaraGuru

ACKNOWLEDGEMENTS

I would like to thank the following people from the bottom of my heart for helping me make this book happen:

My wife, Shweta and my daughters, Radha and Meera: For loving me so much and keeping up with me during the writing of this book and always

All my Clients: For allowing me work closely with you and your teams to solve business problems

All my Bosses: Marek Rucinski, Richard Umbers, Craig Dower, Rohini Kapadath and all others for giving me the flexibity to be creative and think out of the box

My Team-members: Nothing was possible without you

Patricio De Matteis: For inspiring and guiding me

Alex Burrows: For pushing me to write this book

Nalin Tiwari: For your advice on the book
and
Harsh Agarwal: For constantly driving me and bringing life to the book

Thank You all!

TABLE OF CONTENTS

-1-

Introduction

As I like to say, analytics is the most misrepresented term I know. During the past couple of decades of my career in analytics, I have seen so much misunderstanding around analytics that I felt compelled to write this book. After spending years working with something and experiencing its power and possibilities, you tend to develop an emotion for it, which is what happened with my work in analytics. This emotion has been simmering for years, but now it's brimming over so much so, that it is time to start writing about it.

In my global travels working with a myriad of organisations, I've come to see that everyone has their own definitions and understanding of analytics. Perhaps none of them are wrong, but at the same time, all of them are wrong. I see people making Excel spreadsheets while merrily saying they are taming analytics for revolutionary insights. I see people collecting data while assuming they are the masters of the magic of analytics. They are not wrong. They are simply uninformed about what constitutes analytics.

What I present to you here in this book is my understanding of analytics. I have worked for more than 20 years in the field and delivered some world-changing projects with incremental benefits of over $1 billion. This book will demonstrate how to harness the real value of data and elaborate on the fact that having more data is insignificant; what's significant, is your ability to make use of it.

I will share my experiences working with giant corporations. They spend vast amounts of money on analytics, investing mostly in technology and expecting monumental increments in their respective areas, from incremental revenue gains to operational efficiencies. I'll also share how they failed, despite using data and analytics. Let me make it very clear here that these organisations and individuals failed, not the data and analytics. They thought they knew how to use the power of data but the reality was entirely different. And, that's why, with the right data strategies and efficient analytics tools, the same corporations succeeded with better results than they could have expected.

This book showcases the art of possibility available with analytics and how through creativity and innovation, analytics can be used to create incremental business value that transcends imagination to become reality.

-2-

Myths around Analytics

Defining analytics by trying to put it in a box has, in fact, being more difficult than the entire concept of analytics, itself. There are a number of myths associated with analytics which keep pushing people in the wrong direction. Here are some of the myths that people conflate with analytics:

Myth #1: Analytics is an IT function.

Reality: Analytics is not an IT function but IT enables analytics to meet its objectives.

Many companies have put their analytics function in the IT organisation, even though analytics should be part of business operations. This happens because analytics is closely linked with software, hardware and data which are components of IT.

While IT provides the infrastructure and necessary prerequisites for analytics to work, it is not logically or physically analytics itself. The prime expectation from the analytics function is to solve business problems. Badging analytics as IT can limit its effectiveness. Instead, it is far more useful if viewed from a company-wide business perspective. This doesn't diminish the importance of IT in a business; its significance remains paramount in business but IT and analytics have their own roles to play as an enabler and driver of business. We will discuss this at length in the later sections for more clarity.

Myth #2: Analytics means big investment.
Reality: Analytics doesn't necessarily mean huge investments. One can start small while thinking big. They can accomplish much in the process of demonstrating value and creating reasoning for next round of investments as required.

There is not a shred of doubt that analytics demands infrastructure, hardware, software and also human resources. And this ultimately leads to a belief that analytics will solicit the necessity of a huge investment. Therefore, managers remain sceptical about the return on investment of what they consider a major investment.

Another reason that the analytics investment may become a major part of company's strategy is the approach adopted to deliver projects which makes it a cost-centre than a profit-centre. It is not, however, necessary that analytics will always require huge investments to deliver value. Later in this book, we will further discuss how to change approaches, thereby debunking the prime reason for this myth.

Myth #3: Analytics won't tell you anything you don't already know.
Reality: Analytics will not just tell you what you don't know, but it will also make you realize aspects of things you didn't think of.

A business is full of smart individuals and professionals who are equipped with years of experience and have deep insights about the way business or their particular department functions. Introducing a disruptive capability like analytics usually is not able to win over these people, unless well-implemented. It is often believed that analytics is not going to tell you anything that you don't know already. While some of that may be true, another solid contribution of analytics is to tell companies about the things that they don't know already. Analytics helps them find the right questions. Many companies don't know how to ask the right question. While they may not realize this need, it is usually assumed that analytics is not a revelation of new insights. It is rather just reaffirmation or evidence-gathering of what they know or is being predicted.

Myth #4: Collecting more and more data is beneficial for the business
Reality: It is more important to know what to do with data than collect more of it. The relevance of data and the methodology applied to it matters more than just collecting data.

Accumulating data for storage is pointless. Some companies are obsessive about collecting more and more data without understanding what is relevant for them or being concerned about what kind of actions are needed to be taken based on their data. This problem is precisely because of the conditioning done by technology companies.

Acquiring data is costly. Technology companies make good money when they are hired to source data. Bearing that in mind, businesses are told that it is extremely important to have more and more data. While business professionals are unaware of how IT functions, they are sold on storage concepts pitched by many technology companies. Eventually, businesses become obsessed with having ever more data. Hence, this myth has surfaced due to manipulation of the business for exploitation. Even if we agree that more data is really needed, the question is how much more? What is the limit? It is not about simply having more data but with what value you can derive from it!

Myth #5: Analytics needs large volume of data to produce good results.
Reality: There is a wide scope of ways to create new data with what is aready available.

Modelling demands data. In many cases, a situation arises that the data required by the model is not enough. A number of people think this is a dead end. However, new variables and new data can be created by employing creative ideas to match and map existing data with other readily available data sources. It is not necessary that the data is readily available exactly the way we want. In such cases, data manipulation is done to create new data which is suitable to be fed into models to generate useful insights.

Myth #6: The job of analytics is to give exact answers to the exact problems.

Reality: Analytics can also discover other problems and provide solutions both to the existing problem and new ones, too.

It is commonly observed that analytics professionals are approached to solve a particular business problem. However, it is not necessary to confine analytics to solving only that one specific problem. Once the process of analytics is started, new business problems and opportunities could be discovered. The primary business problem might just be a result of several other problems the analytical process is able to discover. It's not about what analytics can find and do in the way of solving a businesses' problems (existing and newly discovered), the scope of what analytics can do goes much further. Analytics can unlock pockets of opportunity for growth and allow organisations to make more money.

Myth #7: Analytics is about statistical models and calculations.

Reality: Analytics is also about integrating the insights of modelling into the business and needs a lot of business understanding.

Analytics goes far beyond statistics and mathematics. To utilize analytics, a very good understanding of business is required. Without understanding the business, it is not possible to understand the business problem or understand what kind of data is required. More than that, the final output of models is supposed to be delivered to the business operations in the form of insights which are written in plain, simple English. Then, these insights are to be implemented into the business. The analytics team must understand business so that they can convince business users that their model is congruent with the business and its problems.

Myth #8: Analytics can be performed in isolation of business.
Reality: Business actions are the critical aspect of analytics, and the agility with which these actions must be taken is just as important.

Analytics provides recommendations on what must be done, and what changes must be made in order for a business to get the desired incremental value from the output of the changes. These business actions are the critical aspect of analytics and the agility with which these actions must be taken is just as important. Understanding the impact to customer's journey is a must, as analytics can help change the customer's experience for the better.

-3-

Definition of Analytics

I prefer to define analytics as a 'Creative and Innovative Business Process' which involves utilising various data sources (internal and external), and applying statistical techniques to solve business problems.

I recommend associating the word 'creative' with analytics because one of the critical aspects of analytics is the *ability* to *creatively* think and understand what kinds of data sources are relevant and what do with them to solve the business problem. Once this is done, they can be ingested for analysis while understanding the output of the relevant statistical algorithms. This will eventually result in creating helpful insights and useful recommendations to alleviate the problems a business is experiencing. The recommendations are to be presented in an easy to understand, accessible way to the business leaders who are going to make decisions based on the analysis. Analytics is not just data, reports and number crunching; it is a very creative and innovative field that requires data, statistics and business knowledge to solve a business problem.

Analytics is many things to many people. Different people have different perceptions of analytics. It is typical that people get involved with a component of analytics and then make the mistake of thinking that's all there is to analytics. On the contrary, there are many aspects of analytics, and many of them are used in small, isolated ways. But those aspects are only a small part of the totality of what is known as analytics.

Let us see what Analytics is NOT:

Analytics is not just doing a mathematical calculation on an Excel report: Reading an excel report and doing mathematical calculations by writing a formula is not analytics, but may be a part of an entire analytics program. Analytics is a very creative process and is much broader than simple mathematical calculations.

Analytics is not data management, data warehousing or data reporting: Reporting may be a by-product of an analytics process. The objective of data management is to be able to collate the information while employing distinct data processing. On the other hand, data analytics is employed in order to be able to reach decision making appropriate to the problem the business is trying to solve. Hence, data management and data warehousing are, in fact, a component of data analytics, but not analytics itself. Reports are definitely a part of data analytics, but they are not the end result or the primary objective. Reports are only part of the process. They help achieve the end result of appropriate decision making for the issue being scrutinized.

Analytics is not Business Intelligence (BI), either: Again, business intelligence is a component of data analytics. Business intelligence is primarily an IT function. It is the set of multiple strategies, processes, data, technologies, applications and technical architectures. These can be exploited to enable the collection, data analysis, presentation and dissemination of valuable business information. Through the presentation layer, BI technologies provide historical and current views of business operations in the form of dynamic reporting, which allows for the slicing and dicing of data.

Analytics is not laying the infrastructure: Infrastructure is the enabler, while analytics is about utilising that infrastructure to lead to better decision making. Many organisations provide the hardware and software for analytics which acts as a backbone. However, the hardware and software are not holistically analytics. They are the enabler.

All the aforementioned components cannot make any money out of data. All these components need to be integrated intelligently to obtain solutions to a business problem which can finally be implemented to make more money.

Introduction to Stories and Segments:

With an experience of more than two decades, I have encountered myriad of business problems. Out of all those, I have selected 5 unique cases that presented a different kind of complexity and demanded more than what can be done ordinarily in analytics. These stories presented themselves at different milestones of my career and helped me revisit and reshape my own construct about analytics. With my brilliant colleagues and seniors, we could ideate and thought shower on the initiated projects to design a path that could solve the business problems using analytical processes. These stories are remarkable case studies that throw a new light on analytics.

-4-

An Olympian Task

I looked at the beautiful Australian landscape as my plane pierced upwards into the cloudless, cerulean sky thinking about my past career and what lay ahead. My entire life had been dedicated to analytics and I've had wonderful adventures in this industry while working for some of the most prestigious organisations. I learned so much from the top leaders of the business world and built relationships with them which I cherish even today, years later. Now, working independently with a small team and I love the work even more.

I was on a 20-hour flight to London to work on a project which included, at least in some ways, sports. In a way, it was kind of my dream project—my love for sports is immense and to work that closely with Olympics was nothing short of a dream-come-true kind of a moment for me.

Sports connect me with the outside world. Had it not been for the National Rugby League (NRL), I would never leave my computer and those data sheets. I like the feel of human metal crushing human metal to exhibit strength and discipline on the field. And, if the Sydney Roosters and the Rabbitohs are playing I never skip the game. Rugby is not the only sport I like, though, motorsports also holds a place in my heart.

The ringing sound of octane burning through those V10s holds an appeal for men that can be found only in extreme sports like cliff diving, or perhaps space travel. Every year for one week the track at Albert Park, Melbourne sends out sounds of speeding cars over a radius of miles. Lovers of Seana, Schumacher, Lauda and Jack Brabham can't keep themselves out of the stands. Cricket. Rugby. Athletics. Football. Tennis. I follow most sports, not only for the physical might involved in it, but also for the discipline sports teach us. How the concept of energy being channelled in order to make revolutionary pursuits possible through mere physical exercises is simply a mystical act.

Working this closely with such a gigantic sports event—The Olympics—even though I was not a part of it in the way I wanted to be, I was still a part of it—making important decisions and developing strategies on how the behaviour of the crowd could be utilized to the maximum for my client's business interests.

I had to meet the business team of a large global consumer goods company, which is a multinational giant with a plethora of products. The team of three people was led by James, a man who had worked for the company all his life and was very knowledgeable and experienced.

You keep yourself to your cautionary best when around such people. The day I received the first email from James, I studied his signature and dug out his history, geography and more. Being in analytics doesn't just give you a drive; it can also give you some really cool tricks on how to find out what you need to know. But it's not just about curiosity. I prefer to read everything I can on the people I'm going to present a pitch. In my experience, there can be 10 different ways of suggesting something, and only one might work for that person based on who they are and their preferences. Something similar to what we do in direct marketing—personalisation.

James had been with this company for more than 15 years, that's what his LinkedIn profile said. Before this, he had worked for another manufacturing company. There was no bio—just minor details about education and his profile in the two companies. It was obvious that he didn't want to waste his time writing useless things on LinkedIn. His position in the company spoke volumes about where he was in his career. The profile was probably just for HR consultancy companies to know that he existed and could be approached for better opportunities.

Checking him out on LinkedIn was only the regular search tactic. As a Data Analytics Professional you can also use what's called 'pipl'. 'Pipl' is a website that uses search algorithms to stream through the invisible internet in order to find information that might not have been mentioned elsewhere on the internet, or hidden from the public eyes. Some databased personal traits mapping is also provided by this website. Thus, having a membership to this site is something a Data Analyst must have, and knowing where and how to use the data given is paramount. I found his personality mapping on this site along with reviews from people who'd mentioned him anywhere on the web. I concluded he was much focused, objective driven, and had straight answers to everything. He was one of those people who would walk out of a meeting without saying a word if he felt his time was being wasted. Presenting to him for someone would be like fire-walking.

I knew I had to keep this meeting crisp and precise. Leave an impact. But most of all not to provoke him. When we arrived, I entered the spacious conference hall with my one of my team members, Sophia. Sophia had brokered this meeting for us—that was one of the many things she was capable of doing.

James was an attention magnet—so much so that I can't even recall the faces of the other three people who were present in the room. He gave me a look the moment I entered. I felt like he knew I had stalked him on LinkedIn. Maybe he had that premium thing and knew who was viewing his profile; whatever it was, my confidence was a bit shaken. But he had no idea how much I knew about him than what was shown on the social platforms.

"This is Shailendra," Sophia said, introducing me to James quickly. James approached and shook my hand with the type of smile that let me know he either thought we were intellectually under equipped and incapable, or he just didn't want to give us this project and was meeting with us just for the sake of protocol. Right there, he showed me that the personality mapping data from my research had been very perceptive. After an awkward silence of more than ten seconds, James started speaking in a coarse voice.

Business Perspective

"The Summer Olympics is only six months away and a million people or so are estimated to be a part of it." He gestured and a teammate of his started a slide with figures flying from here and there. Olympics. The epitome of sports—something that every sports enthusiast looks forward to—not just for the love of games, but for the love of celebrating the games. Every four years, the Olympics goes to a different city which becomes the Mecca for the fans. You can see it pulse with an energy and verve that leaves an impact on all involved.

As I continued my presentation, I started pretending I didn't know these figures. Why? Because in a business meeting where the project being discussed runs in the millions, you can't appear to be over confident or uninterested. I had learned over the years about the art of creating space for wisdom. Sometimes its best not to try to be the smartest person in the room.

"We place a lot of our products at such events. But a common problem that has been reported repeatedly is the issue of inventory levels. Either a particular product goes out of stock within no time at all, or we overstock it and have wasted excess after the games. In addition, the bestselling product or products changes every time which makes it difficult to determine stock quantities needed for the timeframe of the games. For example, during the Sydney Olympics of 2000, we'd strategically launched an energy drink in Australia. Given the effect of its extensive marketing and the tremendous market response we got during the initial days of games, we stocked our stores with consignments of this product. But as soon as the games ended, within months, we had a large stockpile of this product line rotting in stores all over the continent."

He paused and took a sip of water. It felt like he was reliving the frustration of that marketing blunder. Then he continued, "We didn't have any clue what had hit the markets or what made the sales drop so suddenly." They were in the difficult zone of supply chain logistics. This is a tricky space that has been known to make or break the success stories of brands and their products. The supply chain is a paradoxical space that has always bewildered many since it requires maximised efficiency at an optimum speed of operations so that the cost remains balanced with the best output.

Customer Perspective

When he was talking about this particular energy drink, I realised it was the same drink I had tried last time I was at JFK airport in NYC. I couldn't stop myself from jumping in. It was like I knew the answer and it fought to jump out of me, and so it did. I spurted, "Well, that's because the product you are talking about is an American product, a product you launched in Australia after its American success." He looked at me in thinly-veiled disgust for interrupting. I kept talking before he could start verbally lashing me. "When you launch a product during a sports event with a massive marketing strategy, there are two kinds of consumers. The first are people local to the city. Your marketing strategy must have been focusing on them. The second are the tourists who are coming to see the Olympics and explore the new city. The drink started to gain traction not because of your marketing, but because of the American tourists visiting that city for the Olympics who already liked this product and were more comfortable and familiar with it."

I kept on sharing with him. "Americans are crazy as hell for the games and have been known to come in droves to the hosting countries no matter where the Olympics are that year. When they came, they brought their need to purchase more of this product."

I said, "You attributed the sales to your marketing campaigns and expected the sales to continue because of this attribution. However, it was wrong, and as soon as games were over, the sales dropped. People bought the product in Australia and New Zealand because they saw other people, mostly visitors, buying it. The mobilization of marketing driven by sales and not sales driven by marketing made it possible with the added support from American visitors."

I finished by saying, "The surge was short lived because the Olympics ended and the Americans left. Some Australian customers enjoyed the product and remained loyal, but many didn't and they switched to a different product. You sure would not have lost the entire surge in the market of the product after the Olympics. It was the elasticity of the product that kicked in after the Olympics. Am I right?"

"Maybe you are right," James said. "But I am not sure if we have reached the root of the problem. This is just one example and there can be many such possibilities in similar products in the same category!" He was, in fact, right. The energy drink was just one case. They needed a bigger, broader strategy to solve the problem of stock logistics.

"You must predict the demand for this category of products during the upcoming Olympics and stock accordingly," I concluded.

"Not just that. We also need to create a system where we can restock whatever is being exhausted from the shelf swiftly," James added. "We must know how fast it will be consumed in order to manage the logistics." I felt like we forged a small connection in that moment and, for the first time that day, there was synergy between us.

In coming few weeks, we talked many times and exchanged some really long emails, contemplating our future course of action regarding Olympics and our product. James was not the kind of person who would just hand over a project to you, based only on conversations and ideas. He expected some tangible inputs from me, and that's what I did. I worked night and day to understand the problems faced by James and his company. I studied the data of rival companies and compared them with our products. Once I had figured out the problems, I met James in his lofty office and narrated my findings, about the problems faced by his company, to him. He liked my ideas and wanted to know how we would go about solving all the complications. I knew it, at that very moment, that it is the right time to initiate the conversation ahead.

"All the solutions are yours, you know, once I get the project". I said with an air of confidence.

James smiled. "I like your confidence. Let's do this," he said in a calm voice.

Now, to achieve our objective, I had to analyse not just the population demographics, but also the circumstances in which the event was to be held. There were other things to consider, too, from the weather forecast to the journey of the participants and their behaviour! I had to modulate all these findings with respect to various aspects of inventory and supply chain management.

My idea was not just to make a supply and demand optimization model, but also to figure out the exact location of potential stores that could get the maximum utilization of the stock and manage it through demand optimization. It looked complicated, but we were hopeful to get the right data for a concrete analysis and come to some conclusions that could determine how to make maximum sales with no failures. My love of sports and my desire to see the Olympics succeed provided me with a new experience and the games sure deserved this kind of work. I was ready to do it all.

Objective

All companies are profit driven and their objective is to make maximum out of any opportunity. A company wanted to make sure that the demand for the energy drink is met during the Olympics and there is no shortage of the drink when people need it. Demand is matched with the supply so they keep making money with no loss of opportunity and hence, they resort to analytics to predict the demand and know how they can optimise it.

Solution

I was both amazed and excited after meeting James and his team. Even though analytics was something I had spent my entire career working on, I could not stop myself from constantly thinking about the project. Real groundwork for the project started during my flight back to Australia. Airplanes are perfect place to think. Anxiety grew in my stomach. I started chalking out possible contingencies and trajectories to help the big company optimize their business decisions.

Detailed explanation of Analytics Delivery Processes on page 217

I began with my own research about the company and their past business decisions. I was unearthing many hidden treasures: like the one when their previous CEO tried to change the name of the company, but failed to get the board's approval.

Define and Design

I arranged a series of video calls with James and his team to better understand the situation. To my surprise, they were more cooperative than I had expected. James appeared to be a complete sweetheart. Maybe it was just his protective shell that made him look distant. Or maybe he just wanted to scare me and shake my confidence. I passed the test and there was James, answering all my questions with patience and understanding, exhibiting his tremendous knowledge integrated with brilliant elocution.

Once we were done discussing the entire situation, one thing was clear to me: it was a classic case of supply and demand optimization. However, the optimization needed to be done at a very local level for the category of energy drinks.

I made use of all the help I could get. For that, the connections with Sophia came in handy. Late one night I called Sophia over Skype to enquire about some new insight regarding the consumer goods industry.

"Hey, Sophia! So, what is this new thing you wanted to tell so eagerly?" I asked Sophia impatiently.

"Shailendra, it is simple. I recently had a meeting with one of the foremost intellectuals in the field of demand theory and she told me some intriguing insights based on her research," Sophia said.

"The more people feel they are being forced to buy a commodity or a product, the less chance there is that they'll buy that particular product," Sophia said as she related back to me the words of her researcher friend.

It was indeed, simple. I felt like I already knew what Sophia was telling me. But, this simple insight, or you may call it advice, proved helpful in the coming days.

We started diving deep into the ocean of customer behaviour and market realities. James and I met many times during the coming days and discussed our immediate task, Supply and Demand Optimization, over cups of coffee and drinks.

After hard work and long hours of discussions with James, the situation started to make sense. It was especially important to ask the right questions if we wanted the right answers.

I explained everything as simply as I could to James. As data analysts sometimes forget that not everyone is as crazy about numbers as they are.

"James, I think we need to look at this from the customer's perspective. As you know, there are various kind of products in the category of energy drinks. And, local drinks are fairly popular with local people. Then, there are acquired tastes and premium drinks which have a niche market. And then there are several others which are popular in other countries and are available only at selected stores. And lastly, there are drinks that are about to be launched in the coming future," I said to James, who was listening intently.

I kept going. Once I start talking about data and analytics, there is no stopping me.

"As you know, up until now, all marketing plans were based on aggregate data with a bigger picture in mind. But an event like this will bring together an international crowd at the local level, so the need for an intricate supply and demand optimization method becomes crucial," I said. The stern look on my face conveyed the seriousness effectively.

After my conversation with James, I started doing what I do best: working with data and algorithms, following the processes that I have designed over years.

One day, I received a call from the marketing chief of the company. He wanted to know the details of our project. I tried my best to explain to him the workings of our jibber-jabber, as he liked to call our project.

After analysing all the details, I came up with my first idea to help James and his company. The idea was to have a city-centric analysis which could leverage the hyper-local marketing data, collecting the community-based information. We expected performance insights as the output, so that recommendations could be made at the store level itself.

One Monday morning I woke up with an email from James. It read:

"How would this new approach help us? Please explain."

I wrote back, saying "Here the expected benefits are in alignment with the goals of the company. First we will be able to unlock various growth opportunities by de-averaging the city and retailer performances. Secondly, by gaining a better and more in-depth understanding of the preferences of customers and their purchasing behaviour we would be in a position to appropriately manage the inventory."

I further wrote:

"Primarily, we will study the population of the entire city and create a customer profile to know who is buying what and from where, and at what frequency, so that stocking all the stores, new or old, around the venue can be done efficiently. In addition, we'll have a better idea of how soon the stock will be exhausted, so inventory and future stocking can be better managed."

I further wrote to explain the nature and objectives of the project:

"The project will have two components:
- The local population of the city
- The visitors coming from abroad

"Looks very detailed and well-researched. I hope it works," James wrote.

"It will. I am sure of it," I wrote back.

Our city-wide survey had been a success. Later, James asked me to prepare the complete plan and present it to his entire team. He also brought an external consultant to attend my presentation.

Data Discovery

I happily agreed and scanned all my notes and research. I knew that explaining data and analytics to marketing people wouldn't be an easy task. But I prepared my presentation, excluding the technical details.

"Hi, everyone. Hope everyone is doing well," I said at the start of the presentation. "I will directly address the elephant in the room."

After saying some rhetoric sentences, I started with my presentation.

"Data discovery is the first thing we need to do." I said.

"For the visitors coming to the city, we collected data from the last Olympics to discover the ratio of local people to those from participating countries. According to last year's data, there were around 500,000 people who visited from different countries. This number gives us a clear idea of the opportunities which can be unlocked. However, the challenge is to track down the demographics of these people," I pointed out.

"Shailendra, analytics is your swim lane and you need to ensure it works well for us," James said to me during my presentation.

"Don't you worry, James, analytics is my core competency," I replied with business jargon of my own.

We stopped several times during the presentation to discuss various situations.

The fact that analytics is a creative process was reinforced here. We needed help from the semi-structured data of social media to see how many people were talking about the Olympics and were planning to attend. I based my data upon the trends of past Olympic Games. I concluded there was an expected 20 percent participation hike for this year's games.

In addition, a relationship was established between the kind of games and the nationalities they were popular with, in order to use the data to predict attendance numbers for this year. We tapped many other data sources including visas being applied for and airlines tickets being purchased around the dates of the games, and more.

For local setup, a reflex view of the entire city was undertaken, and eventually this data would be fed to the model. For this purpose, we decided to make use of multiple data sources - both external and internal which could evolve to a hyper-local strategy working in multiple dimensions:

Highlights of my presentation were:

- Makeup of Each Store
- Location of Each Store
- Social Media Data
- Understanding the Consumer
- Census Data
- Weather Data

One of the analysts from James' team was really excited about the entire project. The reason was pretty clear to me: he was also a data junkie like myself. He asked many questions about my method and I answered happily.

"So, how did we come to this conclusion about individual stores?" Oliver asked.

I started explaining my methodologies to Oliver and everyone.

"To understand this, the makeup of each store was analysed and the inventory was recorded to see what kind of customers are consuming what kind of products in that particular store. This helped us understand the customer's behaviour better in many ways. Product choices, how often customers buy the products, the changing trends based on temperature and weather. And so forth."

I also explained my methodologies about other parameters: location of each store, social media and others.

"The location of each store and its distance from the stadium was identified, and the average time it takes to reach the store through various modes of transport was calculated. The location of the store in itself had multiple variables, including easy accessibility, available stations nearby, the number of popular tourist attractions and the number of people it would attract. All these variables around the location influenced the percentage of probability of the customer going to that particular store."

Some of the members were perplexed with that much data talk. But, I didn't stop or hesitate. I continued.

"Gaining information from each transaction would have only scratched the surface. There was a prime need to get into the minds of users, and social media is one platform where users speak their mind. We deployed a robust strategy to capture all this semi and unstructured data which gave insights into the lifestyle of the consumer and the city in general. Different polls and questionnaires were put up on all social media platforms to gain deeper knowledge about customer behaviours and patterns. Various deals and discounts were offered to incentivise customers and engage with them through online activities. This provided a whole new side of the customer perspective. There was a need to react to changing trends and for that, it was inevitable that we study social media to avoid misunderstanding consumer preferences and their shopping behaviour."

We also studied travel patterns, lodging details, and a whole host of other individual data to better craft our supply chain management. In a way, it was an all-round Kaizen approach: continuous improvement of working practices and personal efficiency. The flow of consumers to the stadium had to be traced, so data was gathered on the most popular hotels in different budget ranges that would probably accommodate people coming to attend the games. This step was a further filter that helped define the most probable pathways taken to and from the stadium, the stations used, and the bus routes, all of which would be chosen based on the purchasing capacity of the game goer. For example, someone staying in the area popular for budget hotels would be most likely to use public transport to reach the stadium, while someone staying in a high-end hotel would get a cab. The former had the probability to be tapped at the stores nearby the stations with the right marketing banners and the right products."

"We had to consider the things that couldn't be controlled. For example, if the humidity was low, it's very likely that consumers would try to get hydrated, and hence, the demand for drinks would go up. So, we tapped into external data sources like the temperature, weather, probability of rain, any probable infections or minor diseases that could break out, and more. These were all things that would have a direct impact on purchasing behaviour. This data would help to better plan the inventory, campaigns, distribution and marketing strategies.

James was really happy to see the project going in the right direction. He said to me," I think, you and your data will sail us through."

I smiled and nodded.

The last, and one of the most important phases of the entire project was the task of data collection.

James assigned Oliver to work with me and I was delighted with the outcome. Oliver was a talented young man with a knack for numbers and data.

Data Collection and Validation

As per the four broad points mentioned above, data for more than 500 variables were collected and attributed to the following:

- Sales
- Lifestyle
- Shopping Behaviour
- Social Media
- Olympic Events
- Weather Data
- Transportation
- Census Data
- Distribution Network
- Economic Data
- Stock Levels
- In-store Experience
- Promotions Data

For visitors outside the country, the data variables included:
- Last Olympics four years ago
- Countries that visited at the last Olympics
- Games this year
- Number of participants from each country
- Last year's consumption of inventory
- Profiling of last year's visitors

The data was brought together from different sources and a large data table was created where all the relevant data points were consolidated together and updated regularly. Different data points from Census, Weather, Social Media etc. were integrated with that of sales data with the help of the information available on time and location. Suddenly, we had a huge database that transactional information, location, social and product attributes.

Modelling

The first objective was to understand the area and the population demographics. Hence, we leveraged the 73 different critical feature data points which could help us create a very detailed area profile.

After understanding the area, we penetrated to the store level to leverage different key features that would provide a detailed profile of the stores or the brand. This resulted in an accurate, holistic and detailed micro-view of the customers, brands and the stores.

For people coming from outside, we established a relationship between the countries and the games of last year and which game attributed to the mobilisation of people from which country. The relationship was used to predict the profile of visitors for this year and accordingly, their pattern of consumption was traced.

Initially, store clustering was performed to profile each store and understand the sales pattern of the energy drink for each cluster. We then built attribute based regression model that would predict demand by each store during the games. Furthermore, the critical weather data on humidity and temperature was also included into the model to understand the kind of impact it would have on the demand for various products. This would have a direct correlation with these variables.

Once we had an idea of the nationalities visiting and their probable numbers, we started establishing a correlation between the nationalities and the corresponding product availability. The complete stock management was done with the help of these models obtained for different products.

Insights and Recommendations

The business insights that arose from the detailed profiles of the customers and brand were pretty clear. For example, in a particular area, where there was a very diverse urban population—customers responded to smaller convenience outlets in a particular store cluster. The cluster interactions were further analysed to provide even more granular insights about the products and the stores.

We were able to provide a detailed recommendation plan, which talked about placement of stores and the products for both locals and the visitors. The new products were introduced and imported as per the requirements. The shelves were filled, while the warehouses were stocked. We also integrated the real-time inventory data with a centralized server as a feedback loop. It enabled us to refill the stocks the moment they got exhausted and discontinued the ones which were not so popular with the customers. It saved a lot of energy and resources, and as a result, increased our profit margins.

The final output was a GPS-based app, which could provide insights about the demand and stocks and hence, allowed the company to proceed accordingly. The app contained information about the stock levels of the energy drinks category near each stadium where various Olympic events were taking place. The company could predict the real-time consumption of the energy drink based on the profile of the store. When the stock levels were about to reach the 25% mark, the refill order for the energy drink category was sent to the store to get it restocked.

Within the allotted time, we were all ready to make the maximum out of the most massive games on the planet. Finally, it was time for the Olympics to begin, and people from all over the world flocked in to experience the grandeur of sports. We reached to the city to experience the grandeur of analytics and the solution we had implemented. I personally decided to visit the city to see how the app was able to help out. It was working like a magic spell borrowed from one of the Harry Potter books.

The app was being used by the sales manager in the region and the supply chain was optimised to reach a higher level than it had ever before performed at. All the products in the category of the energy drinks could be bought at any time, at any store, as there was a 100 percent availability all the time. As soon as the stock experienced a decline, the sales manager would get an alert on the app and would respond. The app allowed stock levels to be managed based on demand, which meant there was no wasted inventory after the games or lack of inventory when demands were high during the games. Therefore, with the help of data analytics, the profit margin for this product had increased substantially for this year's Olympic games.

I meet James in London again a few days after the Olympic Games. I was visiting to discuss another project with another company, but thought it would be good to drop by and see him. There had been a little communication post the games, as the team had been busy consolidating data of sales to measure the impact.

James was happy to see me. His face brightened as I entered the room and felt the positive vibes around. He got up from his desk and shook hands. Evidently, the numbers were good.

"Any figure, James?" I asked.

"Till they get all the reports, my lips are sealed. But let's talk about what more you can do for our other products," James said.

We had a friendly chat and I gave him more of my hard earned knowledge on analytics, which he listened to like a disciplined pupil. I had become the Buddha of Analytics!

It was time to leave and I shook hands with him.

Then he said, "According to what I know so far, sales have gone up by 220 percent. Thank you, Shailendra."

It was an overwhelming moment. The smile of victory shined on my face. James and I remained in touch. We worked on more projects for the company, moving them along the path of success using a set of variables driven by the powerful engine of analytics.

Key Message/Myth Buster

There are times when the power of analytics will only tell you what you know. What is more important, though, is how you utilize those insights by taking the sort of actions that can quickly and exponentially make you more money. In the above case, the same data was always available during previous Olympics but it took just a little innovative thinking to make a huge difference.

-5-

To Lose or Not Lose Customers

The second important landmark case we worked on was not just critical for us because of the brand and volume involved, but also because working on this case helped us discover a deeper level of the abilities and possibilities offered by analytics. As much as we have worked in this field, the concept of analytics has continued to unfold before us, continually showing us new dimensions that go beyond perceived limitations and boundaries. This project filled us with more confidence in ourselves, and in analytics as a process that can get to the depth of business problems creatively.

The case was truly mind blowing, in the context that it seemed as if the company's trajectory was suddenly under the control of gravity and just started to fall into some 'pit of despair' with nothing to grab onto to stop the fall. Various parts of the company were working in silos but when they were shown the value of the relationship between components, they came together for the greater good. Perhaps this was one of those rare cases where everyone came together as a team while we each put in exclusive efforts.

To gain insights into new technological achievements and socialise with like-minded people, I attend many technology and entrepreneur-related events. Most of these events and conferences are not intensely informative or interesting, but occasionally you get lucky and meet interesting and sharp-minded people that amaze you with their ideas and intelligence. And, at one such event I was introduced to a very interesting person who later became one of my larger business acquaintances.

I met the CEO of this company at an event of the Entrepreneurs' Organisation of the Houston chapter. Even if I found it mundane, I had to be there because of the business-socialising purposes. With a pint of beer in hand, I was observing the big shots of the business eco-system of the city. There were many who flew into Houston for the event. A friend of mine who is a specialist in sniffing potential business out of events like these introduced me to the CEO and founder of a large insurance company in Chicago—Jim. I was impressed—perfect figure and posture, a tailored tux, martini in hand, and an uncanny air of self-confidence which verged on mild arrogance. Heir to a fortune belonging to his parents, but a self-made man in his own right who deviated from the traditional family business of manufacturing and ventured into insurance.

I initiated a conversation. My idea was to impress him with the latest advances in analytics and to show how analytics was transforming every business, and to let him know I was at the epicentre of the revolution and involved with multiple such transformations. But Jim was not interested in what I had been doing with other companies.

"Shailendra, what can you do for me?" He was pretty direct with his the real Chicago accent which is nothing but the typical inland North American dialect.

"Well, a lapidary needs to see the stones before judging them, right?" I snapped back and his firm expression softened as a smile spread across his face. It was not a complete smile. It was more like a here is a challenge smile.

"My guys can surely give you stones. Not sure if you will find them precious or not. Or maybe you can give them a bit of your alchemy to succeed?" He quickly turned around and called for his EA, Christine, to take my business card. I gave the card to Christine and exchanged a smile. When I turned back, Jim was gone—disappeared back into the crowd from where he had emerged.

Christine requested a meeting the next day in Chicago so I rescheduled my return flight to Australia for a later day and went to Chicago instead. I realised I needed help. I couldn't venture into Jim's den alone. So I called Alex, from my insights team, to accompany me. His job is to understand the clients' requirement, gauge it, and then explain it to me in the most creative way so I'll find it interesting. Then, our combined wisdom guides the team. He fought with me on the either side of the bar until we finalized the strategy and chronology of the plan, and then led the project through to execution. He is one hell of a guy. How I met him is another story for another time.

Fast forward two days. Alex and I sat on one side of a conference table. Jim's Crisis Team sat on the other with Antonious taking charge. Jim was nowhere to be found. It seemed he left the matter with Antonious, a Chinese-American guy who had a know-it-all expression on his face. His quirky, untimely smile, which erupted for no reason every now, would make people worry what satanic schemes he was planning.

Business Perspective

"So, as you can see, we are losing customers," Antonious said, "and we need to find out how to retain them. We have the best agents, advisors and experienced insurance professionals, but still, customers are not staying with us. They are leaving us before we can become profitable," Antonious concluded with another unreasonable smile. I mean, who smiles while saying we are losing customers! Everyone was silent.

You see, data analytics is not only a discipline of science made up of only dots and decimals, ones and zeros, the hubbub of machines clicking, search strings streaming through the internet streams and variables swarming around like sharks in oceans. Rather, it's a subtle art where the results have to be shown and presented in ways that can be comprehended best to suit the intellectual level of the audience, or at least appeal to their 'egotistical sublime'.

The interpretation of the graph and the outcomes they were indicating were worse than what we expected to see. All I could figure out was they were not losing money just because the customers were not sticking with them. There was more to it. To sum it up, they were suffering a huge hit; like a pulsating Energon attack in which the next shock wave could electrocute them if something was not done. Having us there was the first step to save them from disaster. But the thing that had been bothering me was not that they haven't done much yet. What bothered me, was knowing that an ultra-smart person like Jim had been so casual about it.

Being in an industry for so long gives you a sense of intuition. You see data as if you're looking at people, they have a 'tell', an inclination. Their personalities, like humans, are inclined to give in to your curiosity if it has been radiated in a specific way to gauge their appreciation, or for that matter, submission. This allows you to figure out similarities, and where the data is heading. Maybe you won't get the exact picture, but the data can still estimate the probable trajectory. It's likely that Jim, Antonious and the others in the company weren't able to see it.

"We will need to analyse all this data a bit, but we can probably get back to you in a couple of days," Alex pointed at their drives in a very professional tone. I was a bit confused about why Alex was not telling them what we were seeing. Telling them right there would have closed the deal then and there. But I trusted Alex and his instincts. Being a team player is important, even if you own the company. Being an owner doesn't mean you are the king in the game of chess whom everyone is supposed to protect. Rather, you are the knight with peculiar moves which can save everyone's job if needed.

"How soon can we hear from you?" Antonious asked casually.

"Soon," Alex said, smiling widely. I know that smile of his. If I wanted to put it in figures, it is 20 percent sarcasm, 30 percent wit, 25 percent frustration and the other 25 percent is unpredictability.

We left and headed straight back to our office to get to work. After some time, after having sat with the statistics team, I could see Alex's eyes gleaming; 'The Tell' as I said earlier. He'd found something important.

"I knew it," Alex said. I look at him, puzzled.

"Look here. They lost 95 percent of their customers in their second year itself! It is so much worse than we expected it to be!" He was about to be doomed and I couldn't resist joining him. Their doom equated to our window of opportunity.

We quickly drew up a report with a short analysis that included the probable problems that were resulting in their loss of customers. With that, we asked for more specific data sets and then sent the report to the Risk Interim team.

Now we had to wait for them to cave in to the cloud of wisdom we'd conjured for them. We provided them with insight into their problem, but obscured the solution so they would need us to help them out. I was amazed how easy it had been, given the kind of organisation and the kind of stigma that it had created in my imagination. A few weeks went by before we received the official confirmation. We started by first laying out our plan and providing an overview to their statistics committee about it. This part of the negotiation was to be in the form of a Skype meeting, which I trusted Alex with.

Everything ran smoothly, and after healthy and regular communication with their business and risk team, we were to receive the data drives along with some necessary logs that we'd asked for on the 15th day of our meeting with the Statistics team. But nothing came through. Alex was not feeling good about any of this so he made a direct call to Antonious. I wanted to contact Jim, but my only way to reach him was through Christine and I knew she would lead me to no one but Antonious.

Antonious: "Hi, who is it that I'm speaking with?"

Alex: It's Alex on this end; I thought we would be getting the drives this week. We've waited quite a while, so I'm calling to get confirmation as to whether we are moving forward or not. I can't have my team on standby for this long for a project that seems to have lost any possibility of taking off."

Antonious: "Calm down, Alex. I think we were clear that Jim simply wanted to see what Shailendra and his team can do for the company. What do you know about analytics? We have got the experienced actuarials and they know far more. I don't understand who gave you the impression that we wanted you to solve the problem for us." I could feel the hidden sarcasm in his tone, diluted with sadism maybe.

Alex did his best to keep calm and said, "I don't know who, but maybe you should check, because all the communication in the past 15 days felt like we were moving forward. Do you mind telling if this is simply stalling because you don't believe in us, or is there something more clandestine and sly you have in mind?"

That was Alex keeping his calm, trust me!

Antonious was equally baffled by this tone of speech. He exclaimed in dissent, "There's no need to be furious about it. You're professionals and this should be understood that we don't want to engage your services."

I signalled Alex to break it off, and at his subtle best, he finally ended the call on a mutually respectable note. I could sense the uneasiness in Antonious' voice. He was pretending to be confident with his words, but he was not. My experiences dealing with such people has given me an indication when they are trying to deal with the problem at their own level and save the fragments of reputation they have left with Jim.

Almost six months of consistent follow-ups and still nothing. Suddenly, one boring weekend night I heard a loud continuous thud at my studio apartment's door. Alex was there at the gate at his ecstatic best. "They've just mailed it in with an apology," he kept saying. I invited him in and offered him a glass of water. "They've mailed in what?" I asked. "The data we were looking for," he said. "A whole Goddamn challenge of almost 30 thousand rows—all uploaded onto a secure cloud! Aren't you excited?"

I was happy for him, he wanted this and now we had it all. Finally, Antonious and their internal team had given up.

The next big question was: how to figure out from what was on those drives exactly where they were losing their customers. But to answer that, we had to map out the complete customer cycle for buying insurance. We needed the map not just to figure out the tipping point, but we also needed it so we could present it to the company a tour next meeting. We were certain they had never done this mapping. And even if they had, we knew we could do it better. So, Alex and I, along with James (my other team-mate from the insights team, junior to Alex) glued ourselves to our chairs to do what we do best: analyse. What came out of it looked pretty simple and obvious, but the data had its own implications.

Customer Perspective

We made up a character called Susan who is simply thinking about getting insured. Susan is the name of Alex's ex-girlfriend. It is priceless to see his face every time I name a character Susan and then say the name out loud.

Customer Looking for Insurance

Now, seeking an insurance policy is something that must be categorized, as not all options available are same. Some are offered as term plans, some provide mutual fund benefits and some are just risk covers, while others are meant solely for tax benefits.

There can be multiple reasons for interest in a particular insurance product, which could be considered the variables we could work on later. As a smart customer, Susan would browse through the products available on the internet to weigh the benefits and what would work best for her individual circumstances. Again, the profile would have multiple variables including her age, occupation, health status, family demographics, different life experiences and more. As per the variables and what may suit her best, Susan would find interest in a specific product.

Now, while she is interested in the product, Susan most likely will research on the internet for available options. That would be a general approach for any informed customer. She can read about various companies that are offering the same product and do a comparative study of various offers that she has in hand now and evaluate them on the basis of benefits she would get out of them. This is one case. The other case could be Susan calling an advisor—a contact she obtained from a friend or a relative, or maybe simply through the Yellow Pages.

The advisor explains about the benefits and also provides her with more options to consider. But Susan wants to take her time. Maybe talk to a couple of other advisors, see what they offer, and determine how secure she feels with each. Taking out an insurance policy is not a once in a lifetime affair. She knows this she will have to renew and pay every year—she understands this well.

She reads more on the internet while the advisor keeps calling her back for follow up. Meanwhile, she also speaks to family and friends for feedback on the product and the company and determines whether she can afford it in the coming years.

Now all of this has to be done in order to create the requisite case lets for identifying the data that's relevant, and those that are not. The continuous data value chain needs permanent data cleaning, and this is the stage that forms the prerequisite for those.

Being a customer

The advisor suggests some really good products, which are in synchrony with the requirement or situation Susan is in. Let us assume that the requirement is related to her primary interest of getting insured in the first place, insured for basic health coverage that covers her family, as well. Selling health cover includes not only the basic plan to take care of hospital expenses, but also other factors such as the provision of tax benefit, coverage for critical illness, funds, partner hospitals, co-pay agreements, etc.

Let's say Susan finalizes a product that has a competitive price and buys it through the advisor. Every year, she pays for the insurance and is living her life stress free as she feels secure about any possible mishap. If one occurred, at least she would be financially secure enough to deal with it because of her insurance plan. Every penny she spends on the coverage seems worth it.

Susan's son suffers a car accident and she is emotionally devastated. She rushes to the hospital with the documents ready. She has already contacted the insurance company who told her they would call back. Susan is at the hospital, but there is no call back. She is anxious and calls the insurance advisor who sold her insurance in the first place. The advisor tells her there is nothing he can do and she needs to coordinate with the concerned hospital. These are the kind of problems customers face. The communication between the insurance company and the hospital was not very smooth, and there was a lot of 'average wait time'. In a time of an emergency, a customer is not bothered about the technical glitches and formalities like 'time in queue' and 'time spent in line'. After a series of phone calls with the company and a lot of coordination between the hospital and the insurance company, things are settled. Susan finally gets an approval for her insurance claim.

This is one of the many possible situations that could have occurred. We mapped out several other situations and the interactions that would have happened.

The factors which contribute to the customer staying or leaving the insurance company depend in large part on this fragment of the life cycle of an insurance plan. This is the stage for which the 'average wait time', 'turn-around time', 'time spent in line', 'handling time', 'time in queue', 'K-maps', etc. have to be analysed in order to formulate the best strategies for keeping the customer. Slight changes in the company policies and operational dynamics change the whole experience of this stage for both the customer and the provider as well. We imagined different situations with these variables to see how each played out in order to understand the possibilities.

Customer Lost

Reality strikes when the customer has an experience in which they had to use the insurance product and they were able to evaluate the pros and cons of the services. A decision is made to either continue with the service/product or not. One day Susan gets a notice to renew that it's time to renew the policy and she re-evaluates her experience and her current circumstances. Over time, customer needs change. They might have found the service below par for a great many reasons, or they may feel they have a need for either a more comprehensive policy or a simpler version of what they have.

Losing a customer can happen for a simple reason such as pricing, or for a more complex reason, such as the average return on investment based on time value of money. In Susan's case, she decides to leave because of a bad experience during the claim. She expected the insurer to be more human and help in the case of an emergency. Insurances are meant for emergencies, after all!

Different customer interactions can lead to different reasons for the customers to stay or leave. For each single possibility of interaction, there is a new possibility for the customer to make a different decision.

Moreover, the process of losing a customer is a complex web which starts right from the moment the buyer takes the product in and buys it. This process, indeed, starts at the moment the sale is made, and the careful or careless deviation of the customer at various fronts of the service are the opportunities that decide the customer retention strength of any company.

Also, retained customers need to be categorized in terms of the lifetime value of a customer, cost of customer retention and quality of customer retained. Customer loss, in its own way, is a riddling genre of market dynamics. This was the reason why Jim's insurance company was losing all its profits for past few months.

This was their problem, and this was their solution.

This same map—step by step, was to be presented at the next meeting with our analysis and findings. Guess who was excited the most? Alex.

We flew back to Chicago for the meeting. I had requested Jim's presence in this meeting. He was going to see fireworks happening when we unmasked all the issues which his team couldn't. I presented the whole idea and proposal which went beyond losing customers. It covered every single aspect of their business, and every single opportunity they could tap into to make more money.

At the final slide, Jim asked me, "So, you mean to say we have an opportunity to make almost $40 million?"

I paused briefly and looked at Antonious.

"I am surprised that you are surprised. Your actuarials didn't tell you?" I asked and left the room, leaving them stunned.

Objective

The company is losing its customers before they become profitable and hence incurring losses. They want analytics to find out the reason why they are losing the customers and what can be done. However, analytics can help to identify the reason behind their losses not just because they are losing customers; rather there is more to it!

Solution

This project was critical for us as we earned it after so much work and patience. We had to prove our mettle and we were sure we would. Fortunately, the company was supportive with data and insights. They worked closely with us to provide all kinds of support, and were prompt with it. As supportive as they were with us, I could not end up liking Antonious. He helped with the right answers but his expressions made him look dubious, as if he was still playing with us. I wish I could see more of Jim participating in this but he had left this jewel in hands of his pawns and had been occupied in crafting another one. That's all they told me when I asked about Jim.

My entire team was extremely excited about this project, especially Alex.

Detailed explanation of Analytics Delivery Processes on page **217**

"I think this insurance project has so much potential. Both for them, and us." Alex said in a very non-Alex-like serious tone.

I nodded with a smile. I knew what Alex said was accurate.

We unearthed many details about their products and customer acquisition strategies while discussing the product cycle of the company with Antonious,

"Listen, Antonious I think your products are good, but the issues lie in your customer acquisition and retention techniques," I said with full confidence.

"Can you elaborate a little more?" Antonious asked. I could see that he was not pleased after hearing what I said.

"Let's get the project underway, and then as the data begins to reveal answers, we can discuss the relevancy and any possible corrections or directions that might be worthwhile to explore," I concluded and hung up.

Define and Design

Alex and I engaged in more discussions and brainstorming. We concluded that the primary object of this company was, just like any other, to make more money in the end. Losing customers was their prime concern, but retaining them was only part of how they could make more money from data. There were three ways:

- Retaining the customer
- Gaining more customers
- Operational efficiency

Whatever we did to help this company would revolve around the above three attributes.

We began by initiating modelling work for the customers who were likely to lapse—which was the primary problem that had started our involvement with the company. The aim for this modelling was to find out why exactly the customers were leaving, and what kind of customer was more likely to leave, so something could be done to stop the exodus.

Data Discovery

Internal data

We started with data discovery and collecting data from the company at the same time to save time. We received all kinds of data from them, which included information about three fundamental things:

- Customers
- Claims files
- Policies

Data for last three years for the three aforementioned categories was received. The amount was enormous, having multiple variables relating to customer, policies and claims.

Business Interviews

While we were collecting the data, we also arranged business interviews with the managers and other key resources in management to gain more insights about customers and the claims, which might not be very obvious from the data. The real-life experiences and insights from people inside the company were just as valuable as the data.

Antonious connected us to the business managers and people who were keeping a tab on what was happening in the company and the way customers were behaving. Even if they didn't have a detailed insight, they at least had an overall idea.

"There are many customers who make a claim, get their money and then discontinue the policy," one of the business managers told us. That raised a lot of questions about the way claims were being made by the customers, which made us realise the process was more complicated than it seems.It was important to analyse the claim decline mechanism to discover how many claims were being declined and how many accepted, and other data around the claim making process.

Additional Data introduced

Apart from the data collected from the company, we started collecting data from many other external sources, which included the census, Stock Exchange, weather and more. Towards the end, we had thousands of variables which seemed relevant at first from different perspectives. All this information was integrated with what we had received from the company.

Data Collection and Validation

We made hypotheses around policy lapses, which acted as the foundation for us to prioritize the variables affecting a lapse. We ran bivariate analysis to find a correlation between all the variables.

The analysis helped isolate the particular importance or impact of individual factors, which helped us predict the probability of the policy lapse. Some of the variables selected were:

- Macroeconomic factors
- Age of insured
- Underwriting outcome
- Agent
- Type of risk benefit
- Claim experience
- Frequency of payment

The set of variables was mixed with internal and external factors attributing to risk, claims and more. We correlated variables against each other and a huge correlation matrix of 1500 x 1500 variables was created. On the basis of this correlation matrix and the hypothesis, we created one large table and these thousands of variables were manipulated into as few as 26 variables. Some of the techniques involved variable binning, data type conversion, lagging to understand the impact of time etc. Each of these types of variables attributed a certain importance in the lapse prediction. For example, risk variables were related to the age at which lapse occurs. Then there were variables like type of benefit, advisor agreement, gender, state and more.

The data manipulation part, in itself, started giving us great insights and we reached out to Antonious immediately.

Whilst we were doing data manipulation, we found out that 78% of their customers lapsed within 14 months of becoming the customer. I asked Antonious, "How much time does it take for a customer to break even with your company?" Antonious turned around and said, "Only after 4years." When I showed him that we have found that 78 percent of the customers leave within 14 months, it was an eye opener for him. This meant that only about 20 percent of the customers become profitable and company's losses were increasing with each passing day. This brutal truth hit Antonious really hard.

The company had approached us to discover why they were losing customers. After analysing the overall situation we found that their state of business was quite critical. We quickly moved beyond predicting, to make a model for them which would benefit the company on three different levels.

I remember a video call with Antonious when I told him, "We can do so much more. There are so many opportunities which we are now seeing!"

The scepticism almost rolled off Antonious, which propelled me to work harder so I could provide detailed insights into what was possible for this company to achieve, and to prove the outcomes were beyond what they could possibly imagine at this point in time."

After further analysing the outcome of the entire data discovery process, Alex came back to me, saying,

"Shailendra, only 15 percent of their advisors are writing a risk of $42 million! That means just five percent of advisors are accounting for 85 percent of the risk in the category! This is crazy!"

I said, "Yes, that's absolutely true but imagine if we were able to understand what these 15 percent advisors do different than the remaining 85 percent and apply the learning to the remaining 85 percent. The impact on the bottom-line will be huge."

This opened up more opportunities. I instantly identified that there was a need for agent segmentation to give us more insights on the lapse propensity. This meant, the first step would be to model for claim decline and the next step would be the agent segmentation which could act as the input for the final propensity lapse model.

"Is there more I should know?" I asked him curiously.

"There is, but I would suggest you wait a little bit more. But I wonder why haven't they invested in the analytics capability which could find something like this in the very first month of their investigation? We found this in less than a week. Didn't we?"

"Alex, understanding data is a skill and not an easy one. You and I are good at it; it doesn't mean everyone else is also good at deciphering the data," I said in a mild tone.

Finally, after absorbing all the data with the business problem in mind, we developed a plan that would not only ingest data coming from various sources, but also outputs from agent segmentation and likelihood to decline a claim. To Antonious, it was gold as we started solving one business problem and were now providing insights and recommendations on two more areas.

Modelling

1. Modelling for claim decline analysis

The modelling techniques included a logistic regression and a decision tree that encompassed many possibilities and possible outcomes as well as the situations around them. The process remained the same. We made certain hypotheses and outlined factors for which the claim could be declined:

- Potential fraud during weak macro-economic conditions
- Type of claim causes
- Time taken to report
- Claim to insurer
- Type of risk benefit
- Lack of education on policy term

According to the hypotheses, the variables were prioritized and the significance of each was understood using logistic regression, which was the best fit model. The results showed that the month of the year in which the policy was the most significant of all, while the type of benefit, reported gap and other factors were less significant. Again, we calculated the odd ratios calculated for the likelihood of a claim being declined. The odds ratio represent the odds that an outcome to occur in a particular situation, compared to the odds of the outcome occurring in the absence of that situation.

2. Advisor Segmentation

More than a thousand unique advisors were taken into consideration, and almost 1.2 million rows of data were used as the input data. It was found that only one percent of the advisors were driving around 60 percent of policy sales.

The next job was to segment this data as per the business rules and in accordance with Recency, Frequency, Monetary (RFM) modelling. Overall, we created four different segments for the advisors. These segments were then included into the propensity to lapse model to understand the impact of various agent segments on lapsing.

3. Modelling for Lapse Analysis

We collected data after modelling for the decline of claim and integrated that with the information we had received from the agent segmentation. This data was tested with three different methods. After some iteration, we found out that the logistic regression method gave the most accurate results to find the propensity for lapse.

The external variables were proportions of: indigenous, unemployed, born in the same country or married. The claim variables and underwriting variables were marked. After that, odd ratios and a quantity were calculated for all the variables. Each odd ratio signified a different situation, and the quantity stood for whether or not this situation would cause the lapse to occur.

We plotted sensitivity versus specificity curve. This model could predict which policies are likely to lapse with a decent accuracy. If had been able to get a cleaner data set, we could have improved the results.

Insights and Recommendations

We were able to group the advisors into four segments:

- Segment A: Best performer accounting for one-third of sales
- Segment B: Worst lapse and claims rates accounting for one-fourth of sales
- Segment C: Average performance accounting for one-fourth sales
- Segment D: Long tail of advisors accounting for one-sixth sales

The business managers had the wrong idea about customer lapse:

The business managers asserted that were customers who would leave after making a claim and getting their money. In fact, this was the foundation on which the idea of doing a claim decline analysis was based. What we found was that the claims really didn't have any impact on lapse; however, the opposite was true. Customers who had not opened a claim for a long time would leave for external reasons. For example, finding a cheaper product. Since there was no engagement with the company as such, the customers felt disconnected and moved on.

Based on such insights, we could finally predict what kind of claim was likely to be declined. This prediction had a direct impact on operational efficiency as the genuine claims could now be paid without investing much effort and the ones which looked like a fraud could be followed up and investigated better.

The profile of lapsing customer:

Another important insight had to do with what customers were likely to let their policies lapse. The profile of a lapsing customer looked like this:

- Younger male/female acquired through a "medium" or "small" agent segment and paying on a monthly or a half yearly payment cycle without having any claims.

- Furthermore, this customer lives in a postcode with a high proportion of people who earn low incomes, or are non-citizens.

Based on the insights, we provided several recommendations not only on how to reduce lapsing customers, but also on improving operational efficiencies to increase the bottom line:

1. Reduce Lapsing Customers

- On the basis of the score for each customer, create a personalised plan for the customers who are at a higher risk of lapsing each month.
- Provide a differentiated experience to the customers who are at risk, based on their needs and desires from the insight findings.
- Each month, run targeted campaigns for each of the lapsing customers to keep them engaged.

2. Increase operational efficiencies

- Only claims that are flagged as suspicious by the model should be challenged by the claims agents, whilst all the other claims could be approved.
- Work Load on call centres went down since they could mark the particular claim as high risk or low risk for it to be declined.

3. Advisors performance review

- Develop a Targeted Training Strategy for Advisors.
- Develop segment specific training. Further develop the segmentation models to include more data and enhance models to include monetary data (e.g. premium and claims amounts).
- Expand models to include unique customer identifiers to better understand cross-sell opportunities.

- Develop succession plan in conjunction with a charter to ensure valuable knowledge capital is not lost:
  » Leverage experience of current salesforce to improve future workforce
  » In-depth profiling of top performers to help in future hiring and training decisions
- Management reporting Implementation:
  » Develop management reports to track salesforce performance along with the tracker on each segment of advisors.

The insights were massive. Even if Antonious had been cooperative, I still remembered the rough road we started at. I am not sure if it was intentional but it was something that had irked me. Maybe I went a bit above the line when I said that thing about actuaries, but I felt I had to.

As mentioned in the story, it was a long presentation. Jim was present at the meeting as well. We showed them that by implementing our propensity to lapse model, the company could increase revenue by more than $16 million. And by using the propensity to decline model, there could be an uplift of $24 million in sales force effectiveness. There was the potential to make more than $40 million. Undoubtedly, Jim was impressed.

I left the room dramatically and decided not to reach out to them on my own further. I was anxious because I had invested too much time and efforts in this but I had to be patient. Reaching out back to them would be simply desperate. But I knew they would come to me. I showed them 40 million dollars and I knew Jim wanted it.

The next day we got a call from Antonious to talk about implementation. Even if I was not seeing his face, I knew his smiles had disappeared!

Key Message / Mythbuster

Analytics is a treasure hunt. You know that a treasure is hidden in a maze and you start a quest to unearth it. But in this quest, the paths you take lead you to many other treasures, at times bigger than what you were originally looking for. In this case, we started solving one business problem, but while doing so, we had to build many other models which, in turn, revealed several other business problems. We provided recommendations on how their solutions could add further value to the company and make more money out of the data.

-6-

Winning the Card Game

After securing and delivering multiple big projects and executing them successfully, I started to enjoy a pleasant goodwill in the industry at an international level. And it is one of those industries where references and goodwill are imperative; they bring most of the business.

Today was just another fine morning and I was enjoying the prepossessing landscapes of Australia—a country where I now feel at home—through the large window panes of my third-floor apartment. I have always wanted to live in the suburbs, a bit away from the chaos of the city. Yet I want the area to be anchored with the required facilities. As much as I am enthralled by the beauty and the feeling of being in Sydney, I never feel full of it, and somehow,

I look forward to absorbing it a bit more with my daily ritual of having a flat-white coffee while reading *The Australian*. But this daily ritual was interrupted by an unexpected call that morning.

The phone call was from my long-lost college friend, Matt. College was probably the last place we'd seen each other, and we hadn't spoken to each other for a long time. I couldn't even remember which city he lived in, the last time we spoke. Utterly clueless, I picked up the call and contrary to my expectations of a friendly whats up with fitting college slangs, he said

"Shailendra, my Chief Marketing Officer (CMO) wants to see you."

I was not just surprised, I was shocked by this unexpected and unsolicited invitation, one which appeared more like a threat. To my bewildered mind, the fact that this call involved a meeting proposal with someone's CMO for reasons unfathomed was so dramatic that I couldn't possibly imagine it was just because I could crunch data. The story of me emerging as a connoisseur of analytics and now working independently must have reached far and wide. The birds might have chirped in his ears too.

I am not sure if my reputation preceded me or this dear friend recommended me on his own, but I was certain it was a good opportunity because Matt could not have been working somewhere lousy. If there was anything to be said about the college-era Matt, it was that he'd kick ass at any white-collar job. Matt was the guy you would resort to when standing at the door of hopelessness. He was a genius. Thus, all we had to say was if there was anyone from our group of friends and family who we thought would one day have 10 luxury cars and get $300 haircuts 10 years out of college, it would be Matt, and only Matt.

I was elated and curious at the same time about this meeting, for a feeling of professional awe had engulfed my imagination as we finally decided on the meeting particulars. I wish we had some time right then for a small reunion conversation, but everything was feasible post the introductory meeting with his CMO, wherein I would be informed about the real reason and agenda of the meeting. The only thing I could get out of Matt about the meeting was: "It's confidential, and rest assured there's nothing to be worried about, you'll be happy to have attended this one. We both value time more than anything else."

We fixed a time and Matt sends me an email with the address and time of the meeting from his personal mail. As soon as I received the email my eyes scroll down to his signature to find the company name. It was a bank—one of the leading ones, and he was holding the position of Senior Marketing Manager.

To be truthful I didn't recognize the bank by its logo or any other detail. But I've been unceremoniously subjected to its tagline on frequent occasions by sales calls for credit cards, bank loans, car loans, and savings' accounts. I smiled to myself as I tried to metaphorically count the number of times I had unknowingly cussed him whenever I used to be rattled by these credit card calls.

Anyway, this made me think a little more about banks and what I could possibly do for a bank; being a data junkie. Curiosity gripped me. I knew banks could find the means to handle their quadrillion tonnes of data, but the question was: What kind of data would they be carrying? I started a quiet monologue with myself to gauge my thoughts with respect to this storm in my mind that one random call had put into motion.

Banks are institutions that generate volumes of data and information every single day. Thanks to the mighty internet, data is being generated now every single second as transactions occur throughout the day and night. At the same time, banks are also vulnerable to fraud and other uncountable risks, which makes the use of technology and particularly analytics more and more important. My best guess for the reason I was meeting with Matt's bank was something along the lines of prescriptive analytics. They most likely were in the midst of an emergency situation that could be harming the core of the bank and they wanted to use external help to debug in the minimum amount of time possible.

I went to Sydney from my home in the suburbs, all through the way thinking about the possible reason for the meeting. I think that's the problem with all the curious people on the planet. Give them a cue and see them dance restlessly chasing it. Exactly on time, I arrived at the bank's majestic building and I saw Matt right at the gate in his banker's armor, a sleek, shiny, Armani suit. He flashes his signature smirk. With minimal words exchanged and as quickly as possible, we reached the 10th floor of the building and entered the conference room which was empty except for the person with whom I was supposed to meet—the CMO.

Business Perspective

In deep thought and equal cluelessness, he was staring at a whiteboard with a huge dollar sign drawn on it.

Gelled hair, wearing a super-light blue-tinted shirt tightly tucked into grey pants which had seen better days and were now exposing different coloured socks and brown shoes—one could say he was a fashion disaster. I remembered to have thought that eccentricity equates to greatness, and that this was going to be a great meeting with a great person and my long drive to Sydney wouldn't be in vain.

"Shailendra Kumar, please meet Jonathan." Matt introduced me. Hearing my full name made me far more uncomfortable.

Jonathan turned back with a smile, and I observed it was a worried smile. We shook hands. He had a tight grip. No words exchanged and we settled down, sitting across the table.

"Shailendra, right?" He asks, staring at me, without looking worried about the problems.

"Heard you have some good credentials in analytics. We have a problem here that we want you to solve."

Jonathan appeared to be experienced and well-networked, so it was quite possible that I was not the first person he was seeing for this problem. It was clear that others couldn't bell the cat and hence there was this apocalyptic sense of urgency.

"One of the products we are desperate to push right now is our new credit card. We are investing heavily in it. But as you know, for every dollar we are spending, approximately half of it provides a return, and the other half doesn't." He looked directly at me, almost intimidating.

"We spend one dollar on marketing: 50 cents works and 50 cents doesn't. If someone could tell me which half isn't working, I could reallocate that 50 cents into what does work and generate incremental results."

Now I understood the purpose of the dollar on the whiteboard. What he said was obvious. However, the answer was not. Thinking about how to get a return for every bit of the dollar spent was driving him crazy. There could have been a problem with anything, a hundred different things could be going wrong or only one of those hundred could be creating all the ruckus. The job sure seemed like finding a needle in a haystack the size of a multi-national bank.

Jonathan explained that they had multiple marketing channels—both ATL (Above-the-Line) and BTL (Below-the-Line). For Above the Line, which directly talks to masses of people they don't know, they had hoardings at the most prominent spots: newspaper advertising, catchy television ads, radio ads, affiliate digital ads and more. For Below-The-Line, which talks to the customers they do know, the activities included tele-callers working day and night, advisors working on ground, exhibitions, direct emails, paid online advertising (YouTube, Facebook, search engines).The list was endless.

Jonathan continued, "The bank has always followed the same strategy of cross sales, discount offers, label offers, pre-approved sales, co-branding options, etc., with minor changes for all of its ace products. To date, this strategy has never failed us. But now we don't know if something's going wrong with campaign analytics, stress testing modules, or the market. Maybe we misread the churn and loyalty data for the pre-launch and thus went in over our head with this product, but none of our efforts are giving us the kind of results we were expecting.

I'm presenting you with the basic version of the problem here, the raw nature of the dilemma that we've brought you in to face. However, the technical details can only be discussed once we agree you're ready to take on this assignment."

Matt, Jonathan and I took a deep breath after he was done with the saga of his problem. Definitely a potential award-winning monologue that he must have been practicing for quite a while.

"And what is your approach to evaluate the marketing performance today?" I asked Jonathan. I felt that perhaps he was about to start another monologue.

"We have overall sales reports and the marketing expenses and then we have individualistic sales reports from selected channels which can give us the evidence-based sales," Jonathan explained.

"Selected channels? I am sure that would be limited," I replied. As strong as Jonathan was, he was trying to hide the fact that they didn't have the right approach to measure the marketing performance and attribute the sales to different marketing channels. I wasn't sure if he had even thought of correlation and external factors!

"Yes, limited. What do you suggest, Shailendra?" He asked. Fortunately, or the opposite, I didn't want to be as vague as he was.

"I need some time," I told him. I had a fair idea of how this could be done but if I was called to solve this, I decided not to speak without doing some homework and research.

"How much time?" He asked.

"I will inform Matt," I said and rose to leave.

The helpful observation I derived from this meeting was that I had to think the problem through from two different viewpoints. Firstly, from the bank's perspective, and then from customers' perspective.

Looking at it objectively, it was a market mix modelling problem and they probably needed a marketing return on investment ratio. But clearly, the bank was not able to innovate something out of thin air to revolutionize the marketing horizon of the industry and turn their marketing bane into a marketing boon.

Strategies, like running new focus groups or bundling pricing, couldn't help them out anymore, either. At least, not without getting an accurate segmentation of consumer base.

One thing that could have gone wrong in their analysis was the micro-economic study of the drill-down reporting of customer for marketing and that might have influenced the marketing outcomes of the campaign.

Customer Perspective

But then again, I recalled the first thought that had come to my mind when I realized Matt worked for a bank; the pain of sales calls from banks. I had to look at this challenge from the user's perspective, too, since they are the ones inundated with credit card advertising.

Suddenly I remembered the first time I got a credit card in Australia. I was not a fan of credit cards. In fact, I was a strong believer of spending what I had in my pocket. The first time I got a call for a credit card by a pretentiously sweet tele-caller was in the office at around 11 a.m. Her words were dipped in honey and then delivered to allure me—I dismissed it right there.

But the way she explained the perks and advantages of holding that credit card, the idea, as much as I disliked it, became a seed. The desire to hold a credit card had been secretly implanted in my subconscious.

During my lunch break, I went out to get some fresh air and saw the hoarding of the same credit card company. It felt like déjà vu. The words of the tele-caller resonated back in my ears, but I was rigidly opposed to having a credit card. I knew I would encounter this hoarding every single day and hence decided to not to look at it at all. It was fine for a couple of days. The idea of having a credit card had started to fade, but it wasn't too long till I saw a contest being hosted round the company on my favourite social network.

"Is it some kind of scheme?" I asked myself. The way I see it now, it was definitely a scheme - the only difference between now and then is the fact that I am on the other side now.

I clicked on the contest link and browsed through what they had to sell. But if only I was such an easy customer. The chase was not over yet. I kept seeing the contest hovering around my screen for next few days and I decided to change my settings so it won't show again.

And just when I thought this was it, half of *The Australian's* front page was covered with this credit card company's advertisement. I felt like it was a cosmic conspiracy. The universe wanted me to own that credit card. It's only now I realise how much effort is really invested to make every single customer feel the same way—that the product they are selling is a God sent for them! The brand keeps tapping their conscious and subconscious mind using a myriad channels.

It took a while, but I finally wrapped my head around the idea of having a credit card while promising myself that I would be very conscientious with my expenses. With this decision, as a smart consumer, I started my research on credit cards and my immediate medium to research was the internet. I recalled the advertisements I had seen and searched for the name of the companies which were providing those cards with those offers. I soon had a list. I did a quick comparison of the advantages while evaluating various factors like minimum repayment, annual fee, charges, introductory interest rates, loyalty points or rewards, cashback and discounts on various transactions.

I was being contacted for follow ups by the companies. I was being swayed by various ads and offers. I was doing my own research to make an informed decision as I didn't want to get into an arrangement that I would regret. The final decision was the outcome of multiple attributes. I filled out the form to apply and the executives got back to me within no time. The period of time between filling out the form in which I expressed my interest, to the time I actually got the card—I think was very critical.

The conclusion I came to when introspectively seeing myself as the customer was pretty clear. There was not one single marketing channel which tempted me to get the card. All those channels worked together to make me recall the brand and the need for the product. Hence, attributing sales to one single marketing channel was not simple. The sale cannot necessarily be attributed to one particular marketing channel.

Also, I was a particular kind of customer profile. There were different customers with different profiles and different thinking mechanisms, which had to be traced out in order for the bank to optimize its investment.

The whole situation was a maze, and they needed an optimized path out of it. It was literally like the Ouroboros ring I had read about; a never-ending riddle where the solution seemed to be the underlying problem of the situation. The winged dragon was biting its own supremely powerful 'marketing' tail by rattling the customers.

I was curious about what had already been done to try and understand how 50 cents of every advertising dollar was failing so that I wouldn't suggest something that had already been tried. In further conversations with Matt, he informed me the company had tried three times and failed each time. The team working on this had been using various mathematical and statistical approaches to find the answer, but were unsuccessful. It's likely they didn't know how to play with the data they had gathered, or didn't understand how the problem could be reduced to a cluster of smaller problems and solved individually. Then all the solutions put together to create the required resolution. They had the weapon, but no clue how to wield it. And wielding the weapon wrong or incorrectly firing it would mean hitting the wrong target. My job was to tell them how to use the weapon they had and what to aim at to procure what they needed.

I took a week to do some in-depth research and prepare elaborate slides, and then got back to Jonathan. When we met, the dollar sign was still on the whiteboard. Without saying much, I walked up, took the eraser and wiped the board clean. Jonathan's eyes flinched.

I presented the entire proposal in detail, clearly pointing out what they had been doing wrong. I narrated the timeline, including necessary activities to turn the tide on that dollar sign. I knew Jonathan would be impressed.

"This looks promising..." he said, hiding his excitement and happiness. I was sure he would be popping a champagne bottle open that night.

"...However, I will give you this project only on one condition."

Time froze for an instance as I started contemplating what the condition would be and how I would respond to it. My instant reaction would get us the deal or it would sway away.

"I will give you this project only if you deliver it." Jonathan and I naturally smiled. I was flattered. Maybe it was Matt who asserted this, or again, the goodwill. Word of mouth is indeed very powerful and I have believed in it always.

"I won't have the bandwidth for a couple of weeks." I bluffed. You have to show them that you are not free to take up any project that comes to you even if you are! Marketing tactics.

"We'll wait," Jonathan said.

Objective

What if there was a magic trick to make your money double for sure? What if there was evidence for this? The CMO of the company invests 1 dollar in marketing but only half of the dollar get returns. He wants to know which half of the dollar is working and if analytics could tell him that. Solving the riddle of the dollar's good and bad halves wasn't an easy one. But the answer was a treasure in itself.

Solution

I had never thought of credit cards this way–until now. The whole experience was illuminating, as well as daunting. *For this project to work out as we want it to, we need a solid marketing plan based on big data and analytics,* I said to myself.

After meeting with Matt and Jonathan, the Chief Marketing Officer, who was frustrated after failing thrice to figure out how, and which part of, the marketing dollar was being converted to sales. One thing was clear to us: The Company was spending big bucks to accomplish the following objectives:

- Better utilization of marketing investments
- Reduce the customer acquisition cost
- Develop a local competitive strategy

Detailed explanation of Analytics Delivery Processes on page **217**

The company had invested a massive amount of money in marketing to enhance their sales, but the basic question remained the same: how much of the marketing expenditure was actually delivering a positive *Return on Investment (ROI)?*

Decisions for marketing activities and investments are usually made on the rationale that the experience of sales personnel and sales reports provides an accurate picture of the ground reality. That's how everybody does it. However, no business decision can be considered complete and authentic until the true zero for itself has been defined. An evidence-based decision extrapolates the probability of a marketing campaign being the most successful with maximum possible ROI on the amount being spent. The evidence need not be statistical; it could be theoretical with staple conditions falling into place for the situation, but some solid proof must be associated.

The competitive products in the market are being popularized by localized provisions marketed by organisations and there is an inevitable need to respond to the same to save the sales of the product.

Jonathan had his own challenges and expectations from us: he highlighted that he wanted reports for transparent and cohesive *Return on Marketing Investment* (ROMI) for all Post Implementation Reviews done at different levels.

While all the respective departments and channels would boast high ROMI, there was no way in place for him to set a universal benchmark and compare them all to get the real picture of his marketing results. While one challenge was to develop a ROMI reporting system, the other challenge was to convince all the product and marketing managers to see the need for it. Come to think of it, I thought that Matt with his Guiana-style charm could always take care of the latter, but the former had to certainly be taken care of by myself.

Before I could start with anything, I decided to start by studying others who worked had on this problem before me. I knew that the company had failed thrice, but I wanted to know why. Matt gave me multiple scoops over cups of coffee on what had transpired before. I could conclude the major reasons why they failed. I narrated the entire story to Matt, who was both excited and shocked at the same time, realizing how sensible it sounded.

I tried explaining everything to Matt in the simplest way I could think of.

"The first time you guys failed because you tried to save costs by doing it internally, which would have worked if you had the right people to the job. Your team had a bleak understanding of analytics, and they were trying to calculate *ROI* by dividing returns by investments," I said in a raspy voice.

"So, is this it?" asked Matt.

"In the nutshell, you can say that. Yeah," I said with a smile.

"Matt, do you remember what Professor Sheen used to say? 'All answers look really easy and simple once you start asking the right questions." Both of us started laughing.

"So, do you want to know more about why your other attempts failed?" I asked Matt.

"One hundred percent," Matt said.

"Your company hired a low-cost service provider to perform the analytics and the service provider started working on it without any clear understanding of the business processes or the statistics associated with it. While there were numbers flying on screens, there was absolutely no cohesion between the service provider and your company. The result was a poor final solution and your company had to write-off some million dollars after the findings were implemented. Not understanding the data is what hit your company," I said.

"You did learn a bit from your past two failures," I said. "Because you finally decided to hire a decent analytics company, but you were too desperate to succeed, and lacked any vision. The newly-hired company focused on the methodology and was close enough, but failed to integrate the insights with the business. Poor execution and, say, poor mentorship. There was never a thought of integration of the model into the real world so they missed the point about how the ROMI could be utilized. The relationship was never calculated, or communicated, with the business. Eventually, the business couldn't understand, and remained under the impression that there is no output at all," I informed Matt in a tone of assurance.

After I was done explaining the past failures to Matt and Jonathan, I suggested some steps to help them achieve what had heretofore been an insurmountable task: A Coherent Marketing Strategy.

We were sitting in a big conference room when I narrated all my ideas to Jonathan and his whole team, including Matt.

"Hey, Jonathan, I think we should start the presentation," I said.

"Yes, yes," said the boss.

I started my presentation with everyone's gaze on the presentation details. Their laptops were open.

"I have read and analysed all the data and I think the situation can be controlled, and we can surely achieve our goals," I said.

"We need to develop a ROMI methodology based on facts and evidence that can be replicated throughout various processes of the complete organisational economy. We also need effective visualization and simulation tools, which are easy to use and can propel business integration."

"Since your clients always have this sense of urgency, with a no-nonsense yet carefree propensity to switch companies, which seems very obvious; we should start small, but think big and deliver some value by the end of the year."

"We also need to incorporate performance optimization techniques with unique econometric models and a project vision encompassing two years which would collectively spearhead ROMI across different products and levels."

"What do you think, Jonathan?" I asked as I finished my presentation.

"I think, it's really great work. Great work!" Jonathan said.

We divided our project plan into three distinct phases and decided to adopt an approach of acceleration for benefit realization. Which indirectly meant our little team consisting of Jonathan, Matt and I still had to show a lap lead to prove that we actually had a shot at winning the race.

Dividing the entire plan into three phases was still an easy job. The difficult part was to get everyone on-board with the project. If I was the captain of the ship, my job was to make every single sailor of the ship feel that it was their ship. I was merely handling the wheel, and possessed a sense of direction and understood the wind. It was up to them to propel the ship. Even if you are an outsider to the business, the inside team becomes your own team and it is important to win the trust of your team which results in confidence and a smoother execution.

But his company had already failed thrice in the past and probably had a diminished level of hope with us. None of them were interested in investing time with us. They seemed reserved and busy, as though trying to ignore us.

Having worked with them closely for so long regarding the data research, you get to know a thing or two about each of the 'Chairs' in the room that helps you to break the ice in such cases. After all, an insight or idea, unless worked upon, serves as an abomination condoning the laggard behaviour and short-sightedness which, in the first place, is the reason for the decline. We started setting up meetings from day one, and after a bit of resistance, we started experiencing some positive response. Eventually, our team merged with theirs and we took all the managers and the senior management along on the project and involved them in each and every step. The idea was to make them realize that it is their own project and that we intended on developing a plan which they not only understood, but also validated.

Define and Design

As discussed in the last section on how analytics is delivered, we followed the same steps to achieve the desirable outcome.

Our phases of approach were laid out as:

Phase One: The premier intent was to provide initial insights for credit cards only, which included trivial details of baseline performance, etc. We were trying to create a space for wisdom actually to pump up the anticipation by giving them a sneak-peek of what data analytics results compared with actual scenarios looked like. That way we could cash in on the anticipation until we were able to unload the real show.

Phase Two: The next step was to perform business integration and employ reusable statistical modelling techniques for benefit realization. This was supposed to be more granular and detailed. Matt and I were to work for this along with various stakeholders and BI teams for the business to make this a seamless process. This was the phase that could especially go haywire.

Phase Three: To redefine the modelling and optimize it further. Also, to implement it on other data sources. More than that, obtain a more comprehensive view of ROMI and optimize media efficiency by media audits. Finally, this was the one in which Jonathan showed a special interest. His MSI GE62 with the GeForce GTX graphics was at our disposal to make the media audits more data-centric, graphically sound and relatable. This was the stage where we cashed in on the wisdom created in phase 1.

Data Discovery

We started by initiating a dialogue with the key stakeholders as nominated by the company along with identified data owners, media agencies, and the product managers. They had been asked similar questions by the in-house analytics team, but not in the way that we did; at least not with the intent that we had.

We developed some questionnaires which could be used as inputs and gathered some high-level data on KPIs and marketing investments that were being done. We asked the right data questions to the right stakeholders. Furthermore, a data availability checklist was prepared which would define the frequency and granularity of the data required.

The next step taken was to do an assessment of data streams, and the granularity, and to validate the formats of data that would be required.

A multitude of data needed to be collected for different information from different sources, like:

- Marketing activity spend for ATL and BTL with finance reconciliation reports for the last three years
- Expenditure on media by the company and competitors by media planners or external research
- Weekly credit card acquisition data for the last three years

- Macro-economic data for consumer expectation index, consumer satisfaction index, consumer confidence index, seasonality, inflation rate and unemployment rate

These data sources eventually resulted in campaign data for ATL activities like sponsorships, BTL activities like partnerships and direct marketing along with weekly expenditures for competitors in media as well as the gross acquisitions for the product.

Data Collection and Validation

Based on the template, marketing investment data, sales/ acquisition data, information about the competition and other data was requested while we did data discovery. During the phase of data discovery, the company boasted about how they had all the data readily available so that it could be fed into the model.

"Our management is efficient. We are very particular about how we manage such intellectual properties." I remember Jonathan saying this.

However, when we really got into it, we realized that scenario was far from the truth. Either they were bluffing or they were ignorant of what real data is. What they had internally was absolutely nominal. Most of the data was with the external advertising agencies they had hired to do the ATL and BTL marketing. I was disappointed, but decided to handle it at my own level and started setting up meetings with the agency, hoping to finally find what I was looking for.

The agency guys were supportive. Considering the kind of business the company was giving them, they had to be. But all I discovered with the agency people was more disappointment. The agency had data, if only it was useful for us. For ATL activities like that of the magazine, they had a list of magazines and the commercials of posting an ad in the particular magazine. They had no records of the kind of circulation and exposure the magazine had! Well, it got worse. This agency had outsourced some of the other activities to sub-vendors, which meant another round of meetings for us. I still don't know how I survived it all, but I did meet the sub-vendors and collected data from them.

The granularity of the data was another major challenge. As per our dialogue with the company, we were expecting data on a weekly basis, but some datasets readily available did not have that level of granularity and hence, the data collection process alone could not suffice. We had to work with the agency and multiple sub-vendors to create data at the right granularity level.

Finally, all of it was consolidated and validated with the help of an analytics tool like SAS. While we prepared an analytical dataset and populated the data quality scorecard, the company officials and participants attended to our qualitative information questions. The final output was a data validation presentation, a data quality scorecard and collated analytical data set profiles. "Viola!" Jonathan said.

From the dataset profiles and scorecard, we found the marketing activities undertaken for the credit card:

- Product marketing, which was spent directly by the company and included traditional media, paid search marketing, digital display, store openings, catalogues and similar activities.

- Corporate marketing, which was on brand, network, awards, sponsorship, corporate image, and reputation.

- One-to-one marketing, which was on email marketing, SMS marketing, website pop-ups etc.

- Corporate affairs, which consisted of expenditure on branding, legal and finance department marketing/projection in government circles, social-industrial setups and public relations to benefit from policy changes.

- Outbound marketing.

We separated out each of them as a separate variable so they could be assessed against the amount spent on them, and the overall revenue fluctuations, while these activities were being done. These activities, while meant to add value, were merely keeping the system from finding better ways to earn some real ROI.

1. Credit Card take-up

We wanted to know how many credit cards were activated against how many people signed up to get a Credit Card. We also wanted to figure out the real-time credit card buyers and the number of customers who signed up but never bought one. We sorted the data on the basis of regions and segregated it on a weekly basis.

2. Losing Customers

The number of customers lost shows us the mirror of the drop-in sales. There could be various reasons for customer loss, including unsatisfactory services, competition, or the capacity of the customer themselves. Of course, the infamous pestering of marketing pitches by various mediums comes into count under this banner; something that had clouded my concepts during the first meeting with Matt and Jonathan. This data, just like the credit card take-up, had to be collected per region.

3. Usage of Credit Card

The marketing efforts made to not just buy the credit card, but also to promote the use of the credit card was also taken into account. It was clear that buying the credit card was not the ultimate game for the company. The customers should use it, and hence, with different schemes and marketing tactics, the company was spending money and trying to make its customers use the card.

4. Marketing

The amount spent on various activities of product marketing:

- Media monies spent that included hoardings, magazines, digital display and television advertising. All of these were collected under the umbrella of above the line activities.

- Channel Marketing Catalogues: How many catalogues were printed to be delivered to various sales outlets or given away to sales reps? What were the other printed collaterals that were being distributed through different channels to lure customers and provide more information about the product?

- One-to-One marketing through sales representatives: Number of sales representatives working and how many calls were being made at the time and how many of them were being closed.

- Direct e-mails and SMS: Used tools to find the clicks on the links that would lead the customers to our website or pages that had further information and call to action.

- Digital Media: Social marketing and ad spend on search engines and social networking channels for potential customers to see and click on.

Brand Marketing

The ATL activities undertaken for the product were also undertaken for the promotion of the brand which would, in turn, have an impact on the sales of the product. The brand marketing happened to have different budgets which benefitted the entire portfolio of products automatically.

Sponsorships

Sponsorships given against visibility of the brand. A comparison was drawn based on the specific stigma of the recognition vs. the traction that it provides. They had consistently sponsored some of the major corporate awards in the last years and the visibility through the same had to be taken into account.

Modelling Process

Before modelling, it is important to understand the inputs we had. After data discovery and data collection, we had our prepared analytical data sets along with the transformation function. My curiosity at the time of our first meeting had swallowed and digested the first course. Now came the gourmet cuisine.

1. Adjusting the Lagged Effect

Something that the marketing gurus of the company pitched during one of our sessions with the stakeholders was that the effect of marketing is not instantaneous; it is not converted to sales as soon as it is done. The brand needs to be recalled, and the memory of the user has to be tapped again and again to finally make a sale. Hence, the effect of marketing observes a lag in its effect which needs to be considered. Therefore, data needs to be refined, cleaned, manipulated and new variables must be created for the same.

The next task was to find the right model that could be implemented according to the business problem and the available data, one which formulated new KPIs and could conform to the older ones as well in a comprehensive way. With the help of the model, we could establish a valid cause-effect relationship that would exist between different marketing activities and the sales of the product.

2. Decomposition of sales

After data collection, we had the following as the inputs for modelling:

- Amount spent for each activity against timeline for which analytics was to be done (3 years)
- Actual sales against the same timeline

We adopted the unobserved component model to do the decomposition of sales. Also known as structural modelling, the regression-based model could break down the sales against the time in different components.

We could hence find the impact that each of the activities had on sales, and hence, the individual contribution to the sales by the particular activity could be identified. Their own data of campaign analytics, which covered the portion of the churn and loyalty data, cobranding risk assessment and other risk assessment modules, as emphasized by Jonathan on repeated counts, could also help us with reducing some of the parallelism errors which could be suffered during regression analysis. It was like peeling an onion.

DECOMPOSITION OF SALES
PEELING THE ONION

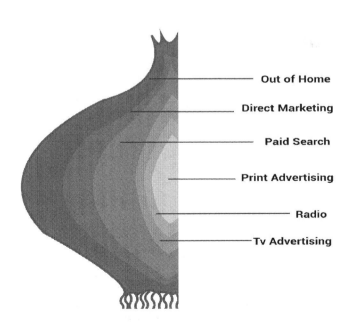

- Out of Home
- Direct Marketing
- Paid Search
- Print Advertising
- Radio
- Tv Advertising

While we did the modelling, we observed that the accuracy level of the model was far lower than we had anticipated. However, modelling is an iterative process and we knew that we had to redo it multiple times to obtain higher accuracy levels.

However, the question was: what to do differently? We had invested enough time to get the right data, got it validated from the client, and the model made sense.

Back to where we started? But again, with the abominable morning ritual of espresso and Financial Review, I read an article on how the economy was recovering from the recession of last years and it struck me how we had entirely forgotten the implication of the recession on the purchasing capacity of the consumers. More than that, we had ignored inflation and many other external data sets like that of festivals, major sports events and many others when the usage goes up. This would have had a definite impact on the sales.

It took us a bit of time, but soon enough, we had more data— all external, though, and after iterating it repeatedly, we were soon at a fairly accurate model—a moment of celebration and joy, in fact! "Viola!" I said.

3. Refinement

Investment versus time curve was made for each activity, and then refinements were done for the curve to bring them into the realistic landscape.

4. Law of Diminishing Returns

While the input (the amount of marketing money invested for a particular activity) is increased, the output (sales of the credit card) is supposed to increase. However, the proportion of the increase in sales with respect to the increase in inputs (fixed as well as variable) might not remain the same after a certain point in the real scenario. Simply said, the soup can only remain hot and sublime for so long. After this point, the level of profits and benefits gain reduces compared to the amount or energy invested. For example, consider a piece of metal that is being hit by a hammer at the same force to be converted into a thick plate. Considering this, we start hitting the metal piece. Initially, with each stroke, the thickness of the piece is reduced by 2 mm. However, as the piece keeps becoming thinner, after the seventh or tenth stroke, the thickness is not reduced by 2 mm. It is now being reduced by 1 mm while the force applied for the stroke is same. The same thing happens in marketing investments, and the sales output of this phenomenon needs to be taken into consideration.

5. Unobserved Components

Unintended consequences: there are certain parameters which would again impact the sales through a particular activity, but might never trigger our awareness. However, to reach a more accurate model, it is important to adjust them into our considerations. These were the statistical unobserved components that cannot be accounted for. This created due to the presence of the brand over the years.

Apart from this statistical unobserved component, there is also another component, which exists in advance and contributes to the sales. It is important to understand this component, which has been created for the marketing activities being undertaken.

Since the marketing was not going to be started from scratch, the brand already had some recognition and the potential market is aware of it—if not fully, then at least partially. The same recognition would help in further sales—irrespective of further marketing activities.

Assuming we had selected data for the last three years, we needed to figure out if we stood at zero at the start of the three-year study. Prior to these three years, the marketing has been done through various channels, and hence, when we examined the data for those three years we needed to adjust the effect of the marketing done before those three years. To absorb the effect of the base, the data needs to be manipulated further before feeding it to the model.

6. Adjusting Base

The statistical, unobserved component summed up with the impact of existing marketing activities constitutes the base which needs to be adjusted before insights could be provided.

It was just like setting a base year for inflation calculations in economics. We set the base terms and counts for our previous performances in the marketing expenditure so that the data generated in the future could account for the measurements with respect to the previous years and also could incorporate the parameters of the same period.

Insights and Recommendations

By making the response curves for resources spent in marketing on x-axis and the revenue attributed to the particular marketing activity with the refinement at y-axis, the insights are delivered to the decision makers.

The said response curves are an input for a non-linear optimization to be performed for finding the range of expenditure which yields maximum revenue. The same process is done for every single marketing activity so that a right allocation of the budget can be figured out for each activity and can be provided as an insight to the company's stakeholders. Final insights need to be converted to plain English. Insights should be defined as clear actions needing to be taken.

The key insights provided by us were detailed to the core. We provided insights on the marketing channel and the attributed sales, but we didn't stop there. We also provided details on the key drivers of the sales and how sales were being consistently driven for every single component. We unlocked the insights which seemed like common sense, but were too uncommon to be integrated into business strategies. For example, we unveiled the figures on how seasonal festivals were impacting sales, and why the curves were experiencing a spike during Christmas. We were able to provide insights about a lot of peaks and troughs in the graph and establish a relationship of these factors with the sales in a quantitative manner.

Business Integration and Action

The analytics process was not complete unless the insights provided were integrated into the business and were implemented further to reap the benefits from it. While we had been taking all the managers and the team of the company along on the project and they were not just informed about each and every step we took, but also involved in it, business integration was still not that easy.

Despite the fact that insights were provided in simple English to be consumed, the client still needs to walk through the entire process and the queries of clients need to be resolved. And they had multiple queries about the insights which didn't appear obvious to them. It is ironic how we do analytics to find out what is not obvious and when we have it, we start doubting its validity.

The process of business integration was eased out a bit for us because, from the beginning, we played smart and involved them in it from day one. Yes, they had resisted, but came along finally.

We explained all the steps of modelling in a way that didn't look technical. Rather, we made it look like a simple theory based on logic. Everything was made simpler for their clearer understanding, and more than that, we consistently sought their opinion and feedback. I already had the salt-and-peppered haired marketing lad on my league, it was the rest of the dwarfs of the Snow White Office (I still can't sink in the feeling of the heavenly white office of the bank when I first visited it) that had to be allured.

After we started getting accurate results, we were able to win their confidence. With the new confidence they found in us, they started providing more business related real-world insights which enhanced the success of model and gave it a real dimension surpassing the theoretical nature of the model. And when the insights were finally implemented with agreements from the stakeholders and decision makers of the business, they knew they had hit the gold mine.

The dollar made on the whiteboard was erased finally. The gold mine they hit gave them an incremental revenue of $32 million every year for the next couple of years. All they had to do was reprioritise without adding a dollar to the existing marketing budget.

How could we win while others couldn't?

Implementing analytics to optimize the marketing investment wasn't any eureka moment. It was obvious that analytics needed to be leveraged to achieve the desired results, but they had failed—not just once, but thrice.

We could execute this entirely because we saw analytics as a complete process and also because we understood the inhibitions and insecurities the company had before getting us on board. We had a clear vision and a well-defined path to walk on while holding hands with the company so that they can match our footsteps and not be left behind. It is, in the end, their business, and we can't convince them to accept a solution if we don't walk with them. Seeing analytics as a holistic process helped us take the layers of this project to its crescendo.

This sure did call for another one of those beer meetings in which Matt and I could add another special glass to our collection. Only this time we had someone else to join in: Jonathan. Cheers!

Key Message/Myth Buster

Business integration is the last but the most important step. An entire analytical process is worth nothing if the insights are not used and integrated in the real business scenario —and this can happen only when you have the trust and confidence of the company in your pocket, because it is them who are going to execute the output and obtain an outcome with the input that you have given them. Involvement of the business is the key to success in any project. We made them feel like it was their own model. As they were involved at every step, and eventually, this helped in the business integration.

"There are things we know,
we dont know
and
There are things we dont
know, we dont know."

Analytics can help you find things you
don't know, you dont know.

-7-

From Internet to Elections

"A 56-year-old woman died in Boorara, Western Australia due to lack of access to a medical facility. Is the government to be blamed for a lack of communication support in remote parts of Australia?"

I remember reading this somewhere long ago on the internet and I could not help but wonder if this was one of the major driving forces for the Australian government to make an ambitious plan for connecting the entire continent with fiber optic cable networks. In the mighty history of public governance, I had never seen any political venture so concerned with the common man that they went on to declare a 'No Death Policy'—that in no circumstances should anyone die because of the lack of internet, or for that matter, any kind of communication services.

I just happened to know someone who was dear to me working closely with the Australian Bureaucrats who were working on sanctioning a new-government-partnered telecom company. My friend Dean was leading the team for supply chain management and a couple of other things.

Dean and I have been friends for a very long time. He was a kind of protégé when he was taken in by the company, fresh at the age of 23, ready to be baked in the kiln of work that was about to hit him. I was his team leader and helped him navigate his way through several promotions in the company. It's not something I take the credit for. Dean was a bright young man and the uneasy professional boundaries of seniority and subordination between us were soon dissolved by spilled beers and some crazy times together. When I left my job at the company Dean and I remained in touch and kept having super-productive discussions on various aspects of the industry. Having a conversation with him always helped me open my mind and think beyond.

When I remembered that snippet about the 56-year-old woman dying, curiosity clouded the thought for a fraction of a second. I wondered what was happening with the communications project and how far along the government gotten on it. Dean had been with them since the project started in 2010, and it had been a year since I'd heard about any breakthroughs or, for that matter, any kind of progress.

Given the timing of upcoming elections, I reckoned at least someone from the government should have been advertising its success. Or, in a not so predictable case, demeaning its failure to gain mileage. Politics is not my favourite subject, but I understand the influence and impact it can have on the market and the way a business can operate and expand. And with this being a government funded company, everything was intersectional here.

I decided to call Dean and see if I could meet him for a beer. Our conversations over towers of beer had always landed on something interesting and I had a feeling I wouldn't be disappointed. And we had this amusing yet interesting tradition for our meet-ups that made me a little more excited about this one.

It didn't take me more than a minute to fix it up with Dean and we decided to catch up in our favourite bar in Australia—The Opera Bar; right infront of the famous Opera House. I have been frequenting this bar since the day I relocated to Australia, and I share a weird connection to it. It's quite nostalgic to visit this place from time to time since this is where a group of fellow students and co-workers had our first ever Yard Ale roundup. It was an epic event that involved some 15 of us who decided to break the record for gulping down the fastest yard of ale, an awesome delicacy of this pub.

When I arrived at the bar, Dean was already sitting at our table with a tower placed majestically in front of him, waiting for me. Blue eyes, bright smile, lean build—Dean has charming look about him which helped secure him a place on the business lead team easily.

"So, what's so different about this one, then?" I asked him as soon as we shook hands.

He knew what I was asking about. We've had this tradition for a long time; giving each other a different glass in turns for each of our get-together meetings. Any kind of glass that might hold some importance, some place in history, or be different than the regular ones provided by the 'house'.

I remember the time when he got us one of those Khantsi glasses, traditional Georgian glasses meant only for lagers. And the time when I'd asked him to get a Pokal from Germany and he went on to get one especially from a shop that kept a collection from the Posen Province of Nazi Germany. He always complained about how hard it was to get that one for me, and I always gave the excuse of how I had to give away my grandfather's Tuglaq coin to a collector to get the Bombard glasses of Tudor-era England. Beer with him had always been fun, and I knew someday this tradition of ours was going to be cherished by other people, as well, once they got to know about it.

"Well, this one is manufactured in Finland, came along with another one, a Sahtirakka; which I'll bring in for our next meeting. Shall we start, then?" he asked.

"Cheers," we said, raising our glasses and started to empty the tower. I sparked the conversation to satiate my curiosity.

"So, what's up with the project? What point have you guys reached?" I asked him upfront. Dean looked at me and smiled slyly. I'm not sure what he was thinking, but it was awkward for a second.

Business Perspective

"Shailendra, when they said we were going to connect 11 million premises of the country with 100 MBPS internet speed by a network of fiber optics in 10 years—which is practically supposed to reach everywhere—I thought they were bluffing, and that it was a political gimmick. But, mate, these guys may seem to be in over their heads nearly all the time, but they were damn serious with this one. While I thought that they didn't have the guts to loosen up funds for such a project, they earmarked almost $42 billion over the years to have a company like this."

Dean can't handle alcohol and you know what, that's the fun part.

"So how many connections are there by now?" I asked, gulping the draught beer.

"Trust me, you don't want to know," Dean said.

"I think I do want to know," I insisted.

"They wanted to have a million by now and you know what our current success rate is, where we stand right now? At one percent of what we wanted! People have a better chance of finding a 'Michael Beer Hunter Jackson's Connoisseur's Glass' anywhere in this world." Dean was fuming by now. I'm not quite sure if anybody but Dean himself understood what that statement referred to, but it was damn comical to see Dean this intoxicated.

He continued, "We tried segregating towns and regions based on their ability in terms of weather, natural acceptability and infrastructural compatibility with respect to demand for providing them a choice between the Hybrid Fiber Coaxial Networks, Passive Optical Networks and OEIC integrated networks. We tried bringing in experts from India and Russia for our supply chain and design chain reference management models. We streamlined the whole process of procurement and maintenance with them, and then we even tried to alter the optical band passes from engineering in order to have synchronous networks in extremely rural lands. None of it helped, and every year met with a disheartened end and hopes of success in the next one."

I started connecting the dots. The government took up this ambitious project to connect the entire country with the internet. This was not just going to help the country, but this would also mean another win in elections. Ambitious budgets were allocated for this ambitious project. The project was rolled out, but it didn't work the way it was planned. It was bad for their reputation, and considering the political climate, it would get worse every single day. They were seriously lagging behind their targets. I didn't know exactly why till then, but I knew I could figure that out. And once I figure that out, I would have to meet the guy.

"Can you fix up a meeting for me with the Chief Financial Officer?" I asked him abruptly. Dean gave me a shocked look. Yeah, maybe I was a bit intoxicated, too.

"What are you going to do? Mate, I respect you, I do! But this is not an analytics problem! Your magic with data is not going to work here!" His hands were in the air while he spoke and I could do nothing but giggle.

"Hook me up. Let's see where it goes!" I cajoled him.

"No, boss, no! I can't go to him and say he should meet a friend of mine who can save his ass by solving the problems that none of his in-house people could, despite having more years of experience than the age of this guy!"

"Dean, listen to me. You have to do this for me. I want to meet him. Trust me with this," I said, and he gave in. Dean couldn't give me an independent meeting with the guy but he promised to accommodate me in their weekly meetings and I was allotted the last 15 minutes of the meeting.

A few days in and even I was curious about what could I do for them in this case. Regardless, I needed more exposure and some opportunity with these bureaucrats and I was not getting any chance of doing that while being a data wizard with multiple private organisations. I needed more challenge in life.

With some notes from Dean, I started doing my research and found that they had divided the entire continent into 1389 pockets. And then the pockets were further divided into multiple Service Modules. They had done some amazing work with dampening the ASEs of the Optical Networks to keep them data loss proof during transmissions. While their technical end was absolutely sound, I found a problem with their non-technical operations.

Customer Perspective

One of the major issues with their strategy was the same data analytics problem I encounter everywhere. They hadn't thought it through from the perspective of a customer. No one can ensure that thinking like a customer will meet the set objectives perfectly, but thinking from this perspective does add value to what you are doing. Since I was living in Australia, I was a customer of this program and so was everyone else. One of the critical factors which I felt must be understood was the placement of the product and where the product is needed most in geographical context. For this project, internet was the product and the parameters associated with the customers' need of internet would play a pivotal role in deciding the fate of the project. I had to think about a typical customer profile who would need internet, and in what urgency. Considering the fact that most office spaces were established with internet connections, I had to think of people who were working from home. That could mostly be women or freelancers and telecommuters if some Australian companies allow people to work from home entirely or even occasionally. Apart from work, families with children would need internet at home. I thought of several such demographics and possible cases and started an extensive research on the possible sources of data and how it could be used to tap into the information I wanted?

Using some tricks here and there along with a bit of thinking I knew what I had to present during my 15 minute portion of the meeting. It could become my ticket to the Titanic. In a few days, I would be presenting what I had in mind to the CFO.

On the appointed meeting day, I arrived at the company's head office in Melbourne. I was led to the meeting room on the 12th floor which had taupe walls and a very ambient feel; there was a serenity in its arrangement. I sat down on a chair located in the corner of the room and waited for the others to come. I'd been told the meeting would start at 4:00 p.m., and exactly at 3:59 p.m., the first person came in followed by a stream of solemn figures representing the Australian telecom industry. Dean was the last one to come in; he was with an amusing looking fellow in his late fifties who turned out to be Mr. William Brown. The room that had been an abode of silence a few minutes ago was now full of chatter akin to the markets of a Malaysian village. I wasn't doing anything but observing the participation of the people, which is a favourite past-time of my job. Since I was already prepared for the meeting, I tried to find out who I should connect with while explaining myself. I could clearly see the characters of this game from my position; the Jim Carey of the lot, the Nerd Worker, the Queen Bee, the Lazy Bum, the three dedicated comrades (more or less looking like three musketeers), the new recruit and of course, the James Dean Bond.

Dean called me over once they were finished. He introduced me to the others and said the purpose of my visit was simply to observe, learn and provide feedback on the meeting. I wasn't quite sure why he hid the real reason I was there.

Now before I could start my piece, the not so smart looking Boss of Dean, Mr. Brown, gave in to his need to state the obvious misconception, "Shailendra, we do not need analytics. This is something different. And even if we did, we would simply go to an analytics company. Not you."

I said, "You have nothing to lose by listening to me. For the next 15 minutes, I will try to explain to you how I can help, and if it is of no use to you, then there's the door and I'll leave through it. A good company always deals from a position of strength rather than from a position of failure. So even if you want to go to an analytics firm after this presentation, which I obviously bet you won't, you might want to go in understanding the problem you are dealing with so as not to seem unaware for not knowing the actual problem you are faced with. So, let me provide you with insight into your problem. You might even have the ability to solve the crisis on your own, if so, I'll be happy to show myself out."

And thus, I started giving them the ride of their life. The ride of logical, technical confluence of facts and simple counting that divulges more than what one can see at the surface and befools the uninformed. That's the soul of data: to find something in its world, you might have to lose yourself to it.

The outcome was that they could reach incremental 5 percent of the population if they used a different roll-out plan. William then asked: "Can you make it better?"

"Yes, but it will cost you," I said.

"How much and when can you start?"

Objective

The Australian government is eyeing a revolutionary roll-out plan to connect the entire country with fast speed fiber optics-enabled internet connection. But the roll out plan was badly strategized and they are far behind from the set target which would cost them more than they can afford. Analytics can help them re-prioritise the plan and help them meet the target.

Solution

A lot had changed since the meeting with the not-so-humble TELCO managers. And now, it was my time to shine with all my knowledge of analytics. The journey ahead was not an easy one, but exciting and full of challenges, to be sure.

"Hey, Dean, let's catch up over a pint of beer," I said over a late-night call.

"Sure, any time, and I've got something you would love," Dean said cheekily.

Detailed explanation of Analytics Delivery Processes on page **217**

"Great, see you then! Good night." I hung up.

A couple of days later, Dean and I met in one of our favourite bars. Dean had brought me the Sahtirakka- a wine glass that he promised.

"You like it?" Dean asked.

"Of course, it's great! Thanks, mate!" I said with a smile.

For the next couple of weeks, we worked together in making this social and truly political agenda the success it was meant to be. There was a problem of not being able to see the results of their technical inputs to the good effort of connecting all of Australia with fiber optics. And it was I who broke the ice and stimulated my own interest stating that maybe analytics could bring in the much-needed solution to this nexus.

After they were convinced that they wanted us to work on this, the office sent their own initial plan. We thoroughly went through it but failed to find a logic behind the plan they had created. Not only did we find it vague, but it looked like a plan which was based on the individual (and half-baked) experiences of the corporate suits from the shady interior of closed conference rooms; instead of an evidence of logic. We were hoping that once we had their plan in hand, we would be able to optimize and re-prioritize it.

Contrary to our misplaced faith, the first look at the Excel sheet containing 3945 rows of areas and 19 columns of variables, gave it all away. The area, population of the areas and other demographics reflected in the document were merely averages with no solid statistical research behind them. It was obvious that there was no effort made to collect the data, leave alone a probability of an analysis over it!

A statistics expert would have one glance at the sheet and declare it a dead end. According to the statistician community, it would be impossible to perform any kind of analytics on it because of lack of data, but that's where the analytics community differs with statistics experts, courtesy of the creative juices flowing in data people's veins. Stats people would say it was not possible because of one simple fact—there were not enough variables and data. Rather than giving up for lack of data, we decided to create data. Analytics, as emphasized enough earlier, is a creative process. And it was, in fact, the test of our creativity for how we would tackle the roadblocks. We could jump them, drill them, blast them, dig an underground hole and pass through right below it or perhaps, do all of these things subjective to the situation.

The first and foremost step was to find the logic behind prioritizing the areas.

After much deliberation with the entire team, and back and forth communications with William, the situation started to come under control.

"I think we are going in the right direction," William said.

"With the right focus and the power of analytics we can nail this," I said.

Define and Design

Over time, we spoke to industry experts and brainstormed with some of the brightest minds of the company. We concluded there were two logics upon which to base the fiber optics network as it was laid down:

1. Ease to Build Method

The concept was to understand how easy it was to deploy the wires when evaluated with respect to the population density, existing construction, new construction rate, growth rate and more. Wherever possible, the network should have been built in places where it was the most 'easy to build' based on these comparisons. For example, if the population density of any area would be high, it would be difficult to lay down the wires and hence ease to build was not in favour of the project. Similarly, if the new construction rate was high, the ease of build will be higher since it is relatively more flexible to make alterations in new construction than it is in older, pre-existing construction. There were multiple variables to weigh against, or in favour of the concept of ease to build. As easy to build as the area would be, the proportion of the speed with which the project could be completed was also a factor.

2. Take-Up Rate Method

As mentioned earlier, the problem wasn't with their technical inputs. Rather, it was with their non-technical operations. In this case, the take-up rate signified the need for a process—that means how many people needed the internet as a priority in an area. A higher priority for user density should guide the higher priority of construction scaling in that area. Despite this not being the premier intent of the project, it made more sense to incorporate this factor, since, in the end, analytics intends to keep people at the heart of it. As experts in analytics, our approach is to understand the problem and then devise a solution creatively, albeit technical or non-technical.

This project was far beyond the data, modelling and insights. The problem statement was not just managerially technical; it was also political. While analytics keep people at heart, people are also at the core of politics. It was a double affirmative, and one that just couldn't be ignored. The solution of the problem statement as a whole wouldn't just be a new roll out plan that would reduce project time. It would be a new roll out plan that would make people happy, and we decided to keep that in the loop at a significant level.

3. Hybrid Method

Dean worked with me on this very closely. While the two logics were thought of, we also decided to overlay the two and make a new plan according to the importance or weight of the two models. So, the third model would be an optimized overlay of the existing two models which we would prepare. We could bring in the practical insight from the data given to us with him at the execution front of this project. And thus, we were able to crack this part of the problem well enough.

We prepared a 5-step analytical process which worked on the same principle of the steps of analytics discussed in the last segment:

- Define the data elements, document them and collect them as per the optimization requirement. In this case, we had to, in fact, create the data and then collect it for analytics to proceed. I still remember the time it took to explain in technical terms the significance of this step to William.

- Score and Classify Nodes, based on Take-Up Rate and Speed to Deploy.

- The third step was to create a new plan on the basis of take up rate and speed to deploy. Which means our ability to replicate upon what we found from the Demand Stats was to be considered in creating the new plan.

- Overlay the two models and assign the score to Servicing Module so that they could reach a maximum number of households.

- Generate business insights for individual models and for the one model which was the outcome of overlays.

- Do the business integration.

Data Discovery

As the sequence of analytics goes, we firstly started data collection for both the methods. Some of those variables were unique to either of the methods, while some of them were common, just reacting differently or similarly to the different methods. After conducting a workshop and talking to a number of industry experts and sitting through extended thinking sessions internally and with the team, we made a list of variables that seemed relevant as per the approach. The idea was to utilise the business knowledge of the seasoned professionals to find just the right variables so that when the modelling was done, it produced the required output and there would be no need to go back to the data discovery phase. The variables were:

Population Growth

Population Growth indirectly links a country's infrastructural demand and execution standards. For this model, the population growth index in the cities could be obtained from the census data. The census is conducted every five years, meaning we had data spanning 20 years. It was found that over the years, new pincodes were being created and cities were being built on grounds and in areas which otherwise had not been urbanized during all this time. The areas which had higher population growth implied new construction, which would eventually require lesser remediation. This certainly helped in reducing some churn. At the same time, higher population growth also meant higher demand for the internet, which implied a high take up rate.

Number of Multi-Story Houses in each node

The Geocoded National Address File signifies every single household in the country and is a latitude and longitude coordinates for an address. A multi-story house is a multiple-storied building and will have multiple addresses at the same latitude/longitude. With a servicing module having more multi-story, it becomes easy to deploy the wire which can cater to more people. The size of a multi-story building with twenty units or more was selected since it was highly probable for them to have common access. The presence of multi-story buildings also signified higher take-up rates in the given area.

Density of Population

Population density had both positive and negative implications. On one hand, it meant that more users could be catered to for a given area and given effort—on the other hand; it meant that the area could be presumptively old, and hence, it would be difficult to lay down new infrastructure. The former factor triumphed over the latter while the effect could be adjusted. The higher density of population would be proportionate to high take-up rate.

Area of the Module

The area covered by each designated servicing module was a critical aspect. If the area is too large or too small, it would either be difficult to build or the returns against the efforts been made would be very low. Hence, an average area would be the best to work with.

Number of Nodes Served by the Servicing Module

As many numbers of nodes are present in a servicing module- it will be easier for the contractor to work with it. Each servicing module has its own set of characteristics in the context of ecosystem, topography, network of people, accessibility of resources and more. Once the contractor is familiar with an area, the work can be accelerated automatically by reducing the time investment in being familiar with local authorities, infrastructure, and other conditions. These were the factors which were evidently visible to the eyes of the execution team but never had been the relevance of these variables been considered by the Analytics team of the company to generate actionable insight.

Regional Metro Distribution

Metropolises have the higher accessibility of resources as compared to the regional areas. More resources automatically imply reduced time lost in shortfalls. Again, something very obvious yet unaccounted for. The clear lack of intent in using data for good could be seen from our revelations. Now, the work that TELCO had done in dampening ASEs of transmission could have been optimized and the effort saved; had they known that Metropolitans didn't need a broader bandwidth for communication.

Servicing Module Distance from the State Capital

This one was deciphered after actually getting inebriated one night while working with the manpower and execution team manager for the company. Matt had brought him over so we could understand the manpower statistics involved in laying down the infrastructure. And overdoses of Cheetos and Carlton Draughts, the manager informed us that cities are always developed outwards from the centre. Hence, the farther out the area is, the higher the probability of the infrastructure being new. Considering the development and the opportunities, the population nearer to the capital would need the internet more than the population away from it.

Number of New Postcodes in the Servicing Module

Again, newer postcodes will have a newer infrastructure, which would help in easy deployment as it would not require to layout new infrastructure.

Data Collection and Validation

After the workshop and the inputs given by the industry expert, the aforementioned list of variables was compiled. The next step was the data collection. While data for some of the variables was readily available, data for some variables had to be created. For example, the Australian Bureau of Statistics was able to provide us with the socio-economic data, demographics data (age, gender, income) and similar other data.

The take-up rate would depend on the population and its demographics. The Australian Bureau of Statistics was a life saver for all the data collection they gave us, as it offered us data on 7230 different variables related to the subject, and it was readily available and updated to the highest levels. However, there was a twist. There was no relationship between the Australian Bureau of Statistics data and the service module data. The ABS data was available at a Central Collection District (CCD) level and not for the servicing modules. Moreover, there was no clear backdrop for why the servicing modules were selected in the way they were, and hence, there was no knowledge of the population demographics.

This was a big challenge for us. We brainstormed for a couple of days to see if we could create a relationship between the two Australian maps and boundaries. After struggling for two long days, I came up with an old-school idea. I remembered my early days in the workforce when there were no data projectors and we had overhead projectors where we used transparencies. If we had to do an overlay, we put two transparencies on top of each other to understand the overlap. That was a good idea to ponder upon, but we didn't know how to execute it. We asked ourselves,

What is a GPS coordinate? How do we define it?

A GPS coordinate is a latitude – longitude point on an x-y axis. With this idea, we formulated another idea: why don't we plot all the boundaries for the Australian Bureau of Statistics data on an x-y axis, fill it with white pixels and then plot all the service module boundaries on an x-y axis and fill it with black pixels. The grey area, the intersection between the two, helped us to create a relationship between the two boundaries mapped on the x-y axis.

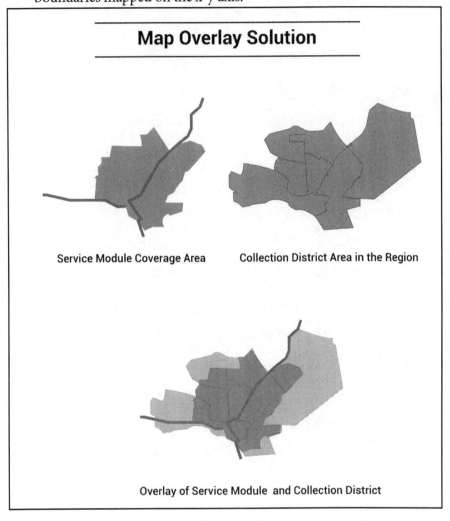

Map Overlay Solution

Service Module Coverage Area   Collection District Area in the Region

Overlay of Service Module and Collection District

Similarly, since servicing modules were not well defined, the number of households within a service module area was also unknown. To figure that out, we decided to use GNAF data for the rescue. We found a subtle way of doing so, by plotting all GNAFs on coordinate axis and also plotting the boundaries of all servicing modules. The whole servicing module was hence pixelated with a number of GNAFs. Overlapping of these plots gave us the number of GNAFs in a particular servicing module. If there was a cluster of GNAF at one single point, it meant that it was a multi-story. This could give us a number of multi-stories in a particular servicing module, GNAF density and data on several other population numbers related variables.

The CEO was mighty surprised with this recent development, not only because his people didn't work this out on their own, but for the fact that despite having such facilities at their disposal, the sophistication was not sought for in the operations. Rather, all the load was put on engineering, field technicians, and supply chain departments while the planning, designing and business integration/ management teams remained in the shadows of the results shown by others.

What we didn't know was the population demographics of the servicing module, but what we did know, was all the required data of CCDs. We had to establish a relationship between the servicing module and the CCDs that were being covered in that servicing module—partially or wholly.

We plotted the boundaries of the servicing module on the x and y-axis first, and then plotted the boundaries of all the CCDs as defined by the government. One servicing module would cover multiple CCDs. While some of them would fall completely in the servicing module, some of the CCDs had only a fraction in the servicing module.

The two graphs were overlapped to find the final area of different CCDs which were common with the servicing module. The CCDs were then pixelated with white dots and the servicing module was pixelated with black dots to define a relationship between the servicing module and CCDs and the data relationships as well.

It had always been about the simpler fact of how many of the users could be using the internet, how often were they using it and what was the proximity of any of the non-users who may want to start using the facility? With clearer, comprehensible, organized and most of all updated data being generated now, the execution of the Take-Up Rate Model had become very easy.

While the pressure kept mounting from the ruling political organisations to report the proceedings and provide the update for the project, we were only halfway there till now. Most of our nights went by working continuously over the data and strategic part, with Dean and William both standing by for my inputs and their approvals. They had provided all the access to the company archives and most of the time one could find me barging into any one of the offices of the department heads trying to figure out one variable or two by talking to them. Looking at the ease with which

I was able to get clarification from company professionals, TELCO had a good departmental structure, one can say.

Modelling

1. Take-Up Rate

However, the data was not in the right form to be fed to the model for the take-up rate. It had to be cleaned and manipulated which resulted in the shortlisting of 2642 variables that were relevant to the internet access aspect. After computing the correlations between 2642 variables by having 2642 X 2642 combinations, we dropped the ones which were highly correlated and were merely agents of multiplicity. Out of the 2642 variables, we selected 385 variables for our regression model to find out the relationship of various variables that drive take-up rate in an area. Finally, we came up with only 13 variables, which were driving the internet take-up and decided if they bore a positive or negative influence on the internet usage.

There were around 13 variables which had a significant impact on the internet take-up in an area. Some of them were surprising. It was found that if the number of widows in an area was high, along with a high population of unemployed males, the internet take-up would be low. Low-income areas also had a lower internet take-up. On the other hand, a higher proportion of post-graduates in an area along with a higher percentage of people working from home and higher income group areas significantly drove up the internet need in the area.

All servicing modules were again classified and scored and it was found out how many of them had a high take-up rate or a low take-up rate. The score could be used to prioritize according to the take-up rate.

2. Ease of Building

For ease of building, we employed rule-based modelling which followed simpler mathematics rules. The model took the data associated with the variable as an input. Now, for each variable, the range between the minimum figure and the maximum figure was defined. This range was divided into several levels and each level had a percentage figure associated to it which defined how important it was. Furthermore, the data pertaining to a particular servicing module could fall into any level. Hence, it would be assigned the percentage as per that level. Furthermore, the variable had a weightage of its own. The weightage of the variable and the percentage importance of the data of the servicing module were calculated to use the score of that particular variable for the particular servicing module.

The same process was done for all the variables, and with simple mathematics, the final score could be evaluated. However, the final score had to be calculated after normalization, because of the variations in the variable that had to be balanced out.

The USP of this model was the flexibility we offered. While these variables were fixed, the weightage of the variable was to be decided by the business experts of the client team. Not just that, the weightage could be changed according to the insights and experiences they had and the model would result in a score between 1 to 5 for each servicing module which would be proportional to the ease of building, with 1 being very easy and 5 being most difficult.

3 Overlapping the Ease of Building and Take-Up models and final insights

The first model produced a score, and accordingly, a priority order to the ease of building, while the other offered another score, and order to the take-up rate. We intended to provide an even smarter solution which could accommodate both the models with a certain level of flexibility.

The idea was to assign a weightage to each model as per the understanding and experience of the decision makers. If they felt that ease of building was something that mattered the most, and take-up rate was negligible as per their own goals and strategy, they could assign a weightage of 1 to ease of build, and zero to take-up rate, or vice versa.

If they felt that ease of building was 60 percent important while the take-up rate was only 40 percent significant to the goal, they could assign 0.6 and 0.4 to the scores and find a new score which would be associated with the new overlapped model.

In this case, we didn't give them any insights. Rather, we gave them an app which was so simple anyone could use it, and it was independent of any technical expertise. Moreover, as more information kept coming from the roll-out happening, the model would be improved further. It was a continuous process— a self-improvisation model. All they had to do was insert data in the app and it would yield the results.

This asserted the fact that was there was no right and no wrong, and the change in variables would result in different outputs. The change in variables would be very much subjective to the focus on the organisation as discussed above.

It had started to look like our timeline had now come in sync with the request of the political demand of this agenda. Dean had told me on multiple occasions how William kept thanking him for having brought me aboard, but I always pointed out that help from any data analytics professionals could have helped them. Things had started to work out a bit and now all that remained was the business integration.

Business Integration

For the business integration, we had a walkthrough of all GMs and AGMs in the organisation through the entire process. Our objective was to convince them of the credibility of the model and the fact that it would actually work. However, it was an uphill task in itself. But, having the full support of William helped immensely to push through our agenda.

One day William sent me an email saying, "We need to do this anyhow for the sake of our future generations!"

Up until this point, I had never thought of my work as something which could contribute to nation building. But, William's email made me realize that the work we are doing was beyond each of us. It had a higher purpose attached to it.

"William, nobody can stop an idea whose time has come," I replied to William, paraphrasing Victor Hugo.

We had more than 25 walkthrough sessions to finally reach a point of unanimous validation. The final app was presented to William who took it to the CEO. But we knew it wasn't as easy since the situation was massively political. When the app reached to the government officials, they denied since it was not possible to get this approved from the cabinet, according to her. We thought this was the end, and all the hard work done in isolation for such a long time would never see the light of the day. When you work on such projects, it is not about the money. It is about the satisfaction of attaining the goal which made you take the first step.

But, we were lucky. Yes, I don't believe much in the word luck but I think the universe could see our misery and wanted to help. Some political activity happened and there was a new cabinet which could see value in the app and asked us to make a new plan. With some more rigorous work and following a similar approach, we could make a new plan which got approved by the cabinet. What followed next is worth noting or part of the success story.

I sent a text "We did it, William."

The optimised models helped to deliver the rollout plan with a further improvement of more than 40 percent and the period was reduced by one whole year!

Key Message/Myth Buster

The unavailability of data cannot be a roadblock to the solution. In fact, unavailability of data is a myth in itself. There is a lot of data that is readily available to be cross-referenced and be used. There are several analytics processes can help to create relevant datasets according to the problem with the help of creative and innovative ways, and that's a key responsibility of an analytics team!

"If you keep on doing what you are doing, you will keep on getting what you are getting"

Analytics can help change the way one does business

-8-

Nothing Succeeds like Success

New workplaces, while exciting, can also make you nervous and uncertain about what the new company would be like. Masking my excitement, I walked into the new office, illuminated with white lights. At places, it was so bright that one could confuse it with heaven, yeah; either I was way too excited or the interior designer was too dedicated to this one. I think it had an engaging smell, too.

I entered this new office full of expectations, aspirations and enthusiasm. A consultancy had approached me to work as an analytics consultant for this company. You feel so important when you are brokered this way—probably one of the very few times when you are objectified and valued, like material things. Another critical aspect of being brokered is that you know you are being brought in because the task is not an easy fix. You know there will probably be fireballs to juggle. It was evident by how badly they wanted me that they were not able to find anyone else.

After a lot of coaxing on part of the consulting firm, I went to meet the executive team of the company who needed my help. They liked me. I liked them, too, but working for them meant leaving my own team for a term of a few years to dedicate myself entirely to this company. I discussed the possibility of outsourcing the entire thing to our team, but they were rigid. They just wanted me, and they wanted me to come and work for them exclusively. Leaving my team was a tough decision as we had been highly successful in the past. My team has always been very understanding; they value experience and enrichment. While me leaving would cost them majorly, they knew what I would bring back would be more than enough to compensate.

It was all good at first, but the company soon informed me that I had no team. Later, I figured out I was brokered to work on something which was supposed to be a dead end.

"What have you done, Shailendra?" I asked to myself.

I had left my team, come to a new office, only to realize later that at my new company, most of the people I had worked with, and supposed to work with, didn't even want me there in the first place. But, like many other past challenges, I was ready.

The day before I began work I got a call from Charlie—my immediate boss with whom I was supposed to work. I was not sure what it was about. When I met him, he seemed like a sorted person. He was nearly bald except for an almost transparent patch of hair ceremoniously fulfilling the duty. He wore a deep look all the time, like he was thinking really hard, his gaze fixed into oblivion. If you didn't know him very well you might find him a little strange. But at the same time, his face was serene—pervaded by a sense of tranquillity and wisdom. After working with Charlie for a while I came to realize he was one of those father figure type personalities in the workplace, the Godfather persona. You don't break this man easily. Every now and then, though, there may be a time when someone would temporarily bring him down, but you knew that all the while, he was silently and strenuously working towards his own resurrection.

I swiped the screen to pick up the call.

"Hi, Shailendra? Charlie here," he said in his firm voice.

"Hey Charlie, how are you?" I asked him, hiding my nervousness.

"Same old. I wanted to call and give you a heads up about a couple of things, okay?" Charlie said. There was no sugar coating. That's just how he was.

"Yeah?" I questioned, trying to sound confident.

"If you are expecting everything set with infrastructure, team, road map and more—just don't show up tomorrow."

I was stumped. You don't expect your boss to call you up and tell you not to come right before the day you are to start. I assumed he was testing me.

"I am ready for whatever is ahead, provided I have your support and guidance," I told him, making an attempt to flatter him a bit. I soon found out it was mere ignorance that led me to say this. In actuality, I was in no way prepared to face what was on the horizon.

"Good then. See you tomorrow," he said and hung up without saying anything, not even goodbye. Initially, I thought he was being arrogant and condescending. Then I thought maybe he was frustrated because of the lack of support from the company. But eventually, I realized that was his personality.

Nonetheless, my first day in the office launched me on a voyage I could never have imagined. I was ushered to his cabin by his executive assistant who seemed to be a lovely lady. Charlie was gazing out the massive windows of the office on the twenty-third floor, unmoved by my presence. I stood for a bit waiting for him to notice, but he didn't seem to care that I was there.

"Hello?" I finally made the move and he turned back towards me. I could feel an energy around him.

"Shailendra…" He came to shake my hand and then gestured for me to sit.

"…Who do you think I am?" He asked. I was baffled. Was the interview round not over yet?

"You are Charlie. You are heading marketing and sales?"

"Yes, I am Charlie, Shailendra. But I am nothing more than the victim of a wreckage, and people are most likely waiting for me to die."

He took a dramatic pause and stared right at my face. Not really waiting for my reaction, he continued, "This used to be a New Zealand company. When the Australian retail tycoon took over they tried to pay me some respect by keeping me in the senior management of the company. Bravo! But clearly, they don't like me. I mean, they can't. They don't know. It's not their mistake, but neither is it mine. I was the COO of the original company, and now here I am General Manager for buying and marketing. It is not my field really, but I am willing to turn it all around. And what do I get to work with? A loyalty program they are now launching! They are waiting for me to give up after getting frustrated, and resign. They can't hunt me down, so they are simply cornering me, waiting for me to suffocate and die. But you know what, we are going to change this."

The dialogue was full of metaphors. I like people with such depth of thoughts, who can observe, relate and reinterpret.

After a brief discussion, we mutually decided to work on discovering a strategy for how to make money from the existing data of the loyalty program. It didn't take us much time to conclude the discussion, and I was relieved to know that Charlie and I were on the same wavelength, at least when it came to ideating. You don't usually find synchronous minds at your workplace on the first day.

We invested some time on developing a strategy, and eventually decided on our approach. I was happy to have access to data for two million customers, which could give me insights on their purchasing behaviour. Everything was perfect, but only theoretically. Now, the actual task of making our design into reality was about to begin.

The practical problem was—not one single Business Manager, not one of our own people—was willing to lend us the product to implement our strategy. And perhaps that was the plan all along—to let us work on strategy, but provide no support or platform to work upon so that we eventually had to give up.

I hate to think this, but I was stuck in between the power plays of the new and the old hierarchy of the company without having any inclination where either of the sides stood. All of this for my first day on the job. I expressed my frustration to Charlie even though I knew he was more frustrated than I would ever be about this. But he didn't wear an 'I told you so' smirk; he was just driven internally by a burning desire to somehow make it work. He told me something that has now become one of the mantras of my professional life. Charlie said,

"Shailendra, nothing succeeds like success."

What we needed was one single success with one single product and that would at least start our journey. It required being patient. God couldn't be so unjust as to provide a strong database of more than two million people who were signed up for a loyalty program and then prevent us from doing anything with it! Yes, God's hand works in mysterious ways, even in big corporations!

One day I was in the IT division, I heard this voice behind my back.

"I think you made a mistake coming here," Brian said, an engineer in the IT division.

"Let me worry about that and you do your job," I said. I was agitated with this but I knew I had to keep patience and the results would soon do the talking.

I had many such conversations with different people in the company who thought that I made a mistake leaving my team and coming here. But, I was sure of the power of data and held my ground.

Business Perspective

And then the company experienced a major setback in one of its bestselling products—meat. The meat was found to contain chemicals. Purchases dropped off rapidly. It was as if we'd been in a dark, cold room for months and suddenly a window opened so the sun could shine in. This was our window of opportunity.

The meat-processing quality teams, despite revamping the production units and supply techniques, were not able to induce the same trust consumers had enjoyed earlier with the product. This was the job of the Marketing and Business Development teams, but then again, they didn't have what we had, the database and research to know how the buying patterns of the people could be used to move the company out of this sand trap.

I went back to Charlie and told him we finally had a product to work on. Even if this product was in some deep trouble, at least we had something to work on.

"You do what you think is best for the company," Charlie said.

"Always," I replied.

I tried to explain my strategy to Charlie.

"What we need to do is work with the database of two million people from the Customer Loyalty program and figure out a way to use the strategy we developed to influence customers to begin purchasing meat again." Charlie was ecstatic about the opportunity that had presented itself to us. He and I were able to crunch the data for the meat business, and within a few hours of starting, we had all the ammo we needed.

"But the solutions need to be creative. Regaining a customer is far more difficult than acquiring a new one. The new customer comes with a fresh slate and you can write whatever you want. Contrarily, a previous customer's slate is full of past experiences. You must dust it all off and write afresh—neat and clean." I tried to sum it all up in a plain language.

Customer Perspective

The first and foremost step that has always worked for me was to think like a customer, so I implemented the same approach with this project. I imagined my wife as one of the customers of the company in order to trace a customer journey using a specific customer profile. I implemented her traits and behaviours into the customer journey. My wife, as beautiful as she is, is also very easy going. She doesn't like the hassle of small things in life like grocery shopping and prefers to focus on bigger ideas. When she read about the chemicals in the meat in the morning newspaper after dropping our daughters at school she was annoyed. Now she will have to go to the other store, which means changing the route she normally takes from school to home. Or maybe she will call me to get the meat from somewhere else and still buy the rest of the stuff from the same company.

At the same time, a smart person like her is now suspicious of almost everything that the same store is selling. Be it bread or any other deli product.

If they can mess up meat, they can really mess up anything!

I imagined her telling this to me, so concerned and annoyed about this news. And hence, in all probability, she finally chooses to go the other store and complete her grocery shopping, cursing the previous company that messed up the way she liked to shop. She so wishes that this mess up hadn't happened and that she did not have to change her routine and her route. If only a miracle could happen! She wished the company would come clean and put this fiasco behind them in a way that increased her level of trust in them enough that she felt confident shopping with them again.

This kind of thinking made one thing very clear to us: customers were willing to come back. We just had to build their confidence and create a lure that would draw them back. And the same confidence had to be reflected in the new strategy to make things better again.

We met with the marketing head and discussed our ideas briefly about the creative approach we would like to take to measure the impact of the kind of campaign we will run to get the customers back. It was difficult for us because they didn't want Charlie to succeed, and I was an outsider to the company—a consultant on a contractual basis who had no experience of the culture and politics of the company and how people there operated. However, Charlie had learned great insights about this during his little tenure with them. He helped me crack the code, and we could see the look of overwhelming amazement on the face of the meat marketing head.

Somehow he mustered the courage to ask us, "What are the cost implications of applying all these methods to my product? I just want to be sure if you provide me the information, I could take these ideas further, and in a better way."

And while the beast was standing directly on top of the trap we had laid, Charlie jumps in to close.

"The cost will be incurred in the utilization of unconventional channels like personalisation, marketing setup and creating a small team which will develop the analytical model to help drive and execute this plan. "Charlie said.

He continued, "We suggest decreasing ineffective marketing expenditures as well as decreasingthe service cost by 8–10 percent. The decrease in marketing expenditure will offset the cost incurred for the project. The whole exercise will result in an increase in acquisitions, opportunity for cross-sell and allied sales created with the help of partners."

The marketing head was sold now. There was nothing else to do than wait for him to give us the go ahead. But Charlie wasn't finished yet.

"There's one more thing…"

"You guys would need to redesign the image of the loyalty program, in its current form, it's not very modern," Charlie said.

"Sure, Charlie, that's a great idea," the marketing head exclaimed.

As soon as we walked out of the meeting, I asked Charlie, "Why did you ask them to change the image?"

The glitter of Charlie's eyes matched his jaunty step as he said, "It was nothing. I just wanted to check how much the bugger was obliged to have met us."

Later, over pints, we had a hearty laugh about that.

Solution

Be it those hearty laughs or intense thinking sessions, I could immediately connect with Charlie. He was full of passion and wanted to prove his worth to his new bosses and for that, he was ready to take some bold steps. I took it upon myself to help Charlie get his stature and respect back.

For the next few months, Charlie and I worked late nights with a little too many Skype and video calls.

One fine evening, Charlie called me over Skype. He appeared to be sad, albeit tensed. For initial few seconds he didn't say a word.

"Shailendra, you know how important this project is for me. And, I think, I don't need to remind you." Charlie started the conversation with this remark.

Detailed explanation of Analytics Delivery Processes on page **217**

"I know, and I am absolutely sure of it that we will increase the sales manifold. Data is an extremely powerful friend to have," I said.

We worked hard and everybody was trying to make this project a success. It was important to everybody. After spending many sleepless nights and long working hours, we started to see some changes and made some good predictions.

We were making great progress and with every little milestone achieved, I could see happiness and confidence brimming in Charlie's eyes. On the other hand, working with Charlie to solve problems one after the other at the company was a life-changing experience. It was full of insights, explorations and learning that was impossible to realise otherwise. While everyone thought it was a lost battle, we didn't just win it, but won many others after that and kept the company achieving new milestones.

The first problem was the decreasing sales of meat products.

When the meat sales dropped, we dug out an opportunity to show some magic. We finally had a product to work on, but it wasn't easy. Though we knew what had to be done, we had to work on the implementation and effectiveness of the plan. Since it was the first project undertaken, there was no way we could risk a failure. The loyalty program had started the very day I joined and we had some good data to begin with.

Data Collection

The data collection part was pretty much sorted as we were supposed to use the loyalty program data only. There were multiple variables which were recorded for every single transaction the customer was making.

One of the members of Charlie's team sent me a detailed email enumerating all the variables. Which were:

- Time and date
- Item attributes
- Money
- Profile of customers (age, gender, address, email, mobile number and more)
- Quantity
- Loyalty card number

With every transaction when a loyalty card was swiped, the data was being constantly fed to a centralised server.

Another task was data manipulation, and it was to be done very efficiently as all of our future work depended on this. The data collection provided us with a number of variables related to the item, the nature of the transaction and the customer. But this data was not fit for the problem statement pertaining to the meat. We had to find specific attributes to meat and figure out the correlated variables in this case. Some of the variables we worked with were:

- Day of the week variable
- Time of the day variable
- Amount of meat that was bought in a basket
- Basket size

Meat Sales Modelling

We created two separate models to begin with:

1. Predictive model

The purpose of this model was to find those customers who would probably buy meat in the coming week. These models try to predict the purchase decision based on the historical purchase behaviour and demographic information collected above. Many techniques are available to solve these kind of problems, but we tested random forest, neural networks and logistic regression. In our case, logistic regression was selected based on the accuracy and ease of actionable insights.

2. Rule-based Model

The rule-based model yielded the customers who had bought meat from us in the past, but they hadn't been buying meat from us in the last 5 to 6 weeks. This implied it was the non-vegetarian customers who were impacted by the news of meat having chemicals.

3. Overlap of two models

The third step was to overlap the two and have a set of customers who met both the criteria—that is, they would probably buy meat in the coming week and they had not bought meat in the last 5 or 6 weeks. We decided to run the campaign for both B and C.

However, we didn't target the customers who never bought meat from us since it was highly probable that they were vegetarians and it was not appropriate to run a campaign for such people. Even if a segment of customers existed that was not buying meat from us but from someone else, we decided to exclude that segment. Our major objective was not to acquire more customers for meat, but to sell more to the existing customers. Having a clear objective in place was extremely critical to the project since everything was dependent on it.

At the same time, we also had to incorporate the impact of the general campaign around meat that was being run by the company. There was a high possibility of change in the customer's behaviour for meat buying because of such campaigns, and if that was not to be taken into consideration, it would badly impact the accuracy of the model.

Once we had the data for customers who were in B and C, we divided them into two groups. While 90 percent of such customers were placed in the target group, the remaining 10 percent were placed in the control group. We ran a campaign with the target group by sending them emails with a discount on petrol if they wanted more meat. Considering the fact that petrol is a basic necessity and the company-owned petrol pumps apart from the stores, petrol seemed the right choice. The control group remained untouched, so that the behaviour pattern of both the groups could be analysed, and the impact of the campaign could be measured.

Insights and Recommendations

The unique fact with this method was integrating the business rules with statistical analysis to create a hybrid model, which had never been done before. We applied business rules while finalizing the target groups and control groups, and used business acumen as it applied to statistical analytics. We could have just used the rule-based model, but the accuracy would not have been as good as this method.

We were able to score each of our loyalty card customers with a propensity to buy meat score. This allowed us to pick the top ten thousand customers who we could target to increase meat sales. Finding the customers to target was one thing, coming up with an offer to make them buy, was another. At that moment, I came up with an idea to create something that we called "Spend Stretch". Spend Stretch was designed to create personalised offers for different customers who were likely to buy meat. We told them that if they spent an additional $5 on meat, they would get a 10% discount on the meat. This way, we increased their spend on meat and also got customers to come and shop with us, even if they were not looking to buy anything that week. And when they came to buy meat, they ended up buying veggies as well—when you go shopping, you end up buying things which you don't even need.

The campaign resulted in a response rate of more 36%, which is far better than the industry standards.

The success story of tainted meat becoming a best-selling product again spread like wildfire. We were the new heroes of the company. Everyone wanted to talk to us to see how data could be used to increase the sales of other products.

Carlots (local term for truckloads) of spleens, bacon, bile consignments, chops and other items were rolling out of the inventory. Business managers started to understand the power of analytics, even if they didn't understand what analytics was. Following meat, we had business managers of bread, confectionaries and many more trying to schedule a meeting to see what we could do for them. Charlie was happy and so was I. We finally found success in a graveyard. However, the challenge was to go beyond what mere luck had provided us.

My companion on the next journey in this company was George. Irish origins, friendly but always serious. George was known as one of the most committed professionals in the company. Despite workload and stress, his charm hadn't faded away over all these years. He was the kind of person that could light up your day just by engaging in conversation with him. Pressures to increase the revenue towered over him. And so, he turned to the magic of data analytics. Well, it is not magic, but it is a rare combination of art and science, or perhaps, creativity and logic. But to an outsider, it is nothing less than magic, and trust me, at times we refrain from explaining to retain the mystical aura around us—as sorcerers of numbers and data.

One morning I got an email to catch-up from George— an important person in the company hierarchy. He headed the Mobile Products division. However, before we could see each other in the office, I ran into him in the elevator. The moment he saw me, his face lit up.

"I was looking for you, Shailendra. Lunch?" I returned his smile and agreed. At that time, I was not speaking to a lot of people in the company; keeping it a bit reserved for some time. Staying mysterious helps.

We got out of the elevator and went to his office. It was close to lunch time and hunger pangs were taking over.

"What would you like to have? Will a McDonald's combo work?" he asked and then paused for a moment, like he was frozen. I still cannot forget that expression of his—it solidified while time flowed around him. I looked at him in bewilderment.

"This is exactly what we want!" He rejoiced.

"What?" I had no idea why figuring out a McDonald's meal was a jackpot for him.

Business Perspective

"Combinations! They are a huge success. We need more successful combos, and Shailendra, you are going to tell me what those combinations are!" He prophesied.

Combinations were a great idea—no doubt in that. And more than anything, combinations have a proven track record of success. Introducing new combinations was a very legit way to increase the revenue.

It was obvious that rather than doing tests to try different combinations to determine which sold more, analytics seemed a viable option that would offer a logical answer. Analytics could provide one single combination that had the highest probability of success based on past customer behaviour.

George and I spent the afternoon researching the kinds of combinations that had worked in the past. The generic reports and articles provided solid evidence on the success of product bundling for various companies, utilizing the power of data. In fact, some of the companies in the banking and insurance sector had developed robust business strategies around the concept of product bundling which had yielded unimaginable results. However, the concept of product bundling seemed to be mostly successful for the companies which were operating in an imperfectly competitive market. That means, in the marketplace, there was little to no competition for the products. At that point in time, our market was by and large not ideal, but testing product bundling was promising and tempting enough to sail with that wind.

We researched more and discovered that product bundling usually works when the customers have very heterogeneous demands and value the worth of different products differently. An intelligent product bundling cannot only make them buy more, but doing so also provides better margins for the company overall. Bundling could be seen everywhere, from markets to politics. We decided that we could also use it effectively. We couldn't stay away.

Customer Perspective

For customers, it was just as much of a victory as it was for the company. Understanding the customers' point of view—if we offered them all that they wanted to buy anyway, with a discount, the buying probability would go much higher.

At the same time, if they saw a discount on one of the leading products that they absolutely wanted to buy, and there was a secondary product in bundle, they wouldn't mind getting it, too. This would give the company a chance to push the secondary product and let the customers develop a taste for it.

Each bundle of products would draw a different reaction from customers based on the nature of the bundle, and on their preferences. Multiple possibilities could surface in relation to the buying behaviour over the product bundling concept. But what we needed immediately was one single combination that could give us a sure shot at success.

We talked more about the possibilities and combinations, which seemed obvious, but what eventually happened was beyond obvious. Interesting discoveries and identifying opportunities—there was so much more that analytics helped us know.

The random encounter with George and a brief conversation we had in the lift gave me something new to work on— increasing the revenue of the company by making customers buy more.

George was clear about his demands. He wanted to increase sales and revenues.

George asked me to give my hundred percent. To use his exact words, he said, "I don't want any problems with my work. I am expecting you on your best game."

"I always do my best," I said, my eyes beaming with confidence. If there is something I am confident about, it is my work and what I can do.

I knew that the need for making combinations was legit, and it had been, in fact, a tried and tested method to increase sales. Be it McDonald's or any other company, combos have always been bestselling items and lucrative for the customers. Making a combination of products was a classic case of market basket analysis.

One evening George asked me to join him in his office. He wanted to inquire about the entire process.

"The concept is simple; it aims to find if there are several products which are usually bought together repeatedly. For example, if a customer is buying flour and casting sugar, you can see that they are also buying eggs, since, most probably, they are baking a cake, and all of these items are the basic ingredients for the same," I said.

"We applied the rules of association analysis which is used to discover hidden relationships between various products. The relationships might not look too obvious, but are usually solid and they have a rationality behind them. The output also might look suspicious, because at times, they occur out of sheer chance, but if the relationship can be validated with an external rule, they make complete sense."

I could see George was pretty excited about all of this.

As was the case in other projects, we followed the same approach which included:

Data collection

The source of data was the same—that was the loyalty program which gave us a wide range of variables to pick from. We decided to go with the following variables which seemed useful from my own expertise and the understanding of the company:

- Date and time
- Quantity
- Item id
- Price
- Transaction information
- Customer information
- Category information

With these variables and a bit of manipulation, we created models at two different levels:

Modelling for combination

1. Transactional Model

This was a typical association analysis problem using the transaction id. Association analysis has been around for a long time and a lot of retailers use it for creating combinations by discovering interesting relationships hidden in large datasets. Association analysis was used in this case to understand which two products were being sold together repeatedly in one single transaction.

Solving this at a transactional level wouldn't have helped us as it doesn't give us time to act. Through this model, we found out what two products are bought together, but we wanted to know what two products are sold with a time gap.

2. Customer Model

The customer model identified two products which a customer bought repeatedly within a time period of one day. It was important to impose a time frame here, otherwise, there were possibilities of the time difference being too long to make any sense and it would not allow room for any action. This was a sequential model—which meant that it was not necessary that the said two products were bought in one single transaction. It could be bought after some time, but within one day. Since the stores were conveniently located near to suburbs, it was easy for the residents to walk down to the store multiple times and make multiple transactions.

Insights and Recommendations

We analysed all the transactions and the results were a bit unexpected and astonishing. One of the major revelations of the analysis was that liquor and mobile phone recharge were being bought together heavily in both the models. I presented the data to George, but he didn't seem convinced as there was absolutely no relationship between them. Snacks and munchies were the most expected products to be bought with liquor, but recharge seemed beyond reason.

It wasn't too late before I could experience the relationship between the two on my own. Call it serendipity or something. I was returning home in suburbs from the city and was happy high as I reminded myself that the missus and kids were away for the weekend. As I reached home, I had a beer and then the next one, but with each additional stubby my desire to strike a conversation increased. I felt like talking; so, I ended up calling a few friends. The next morning, I discovered my tendency to converse when I am drunk. Mostly I am a social drinker; therefore, I always have folks around me to talk to while I drink thus no need to call people on their mobile for a Chat. But this is not the case with the entire population every night. I was having an epiphany along with the hangover—people like to talk while enjoying their drink! May it be in person or over the phone. But as strongly as I felt about it, it was still a personal experience. Drunk talk is common—no doubts about that, but I needed proof.

I started researching on my phone, and there you go! It was not an analytics problem anymore, it was psychology. There were a number of articles enforcing why people like to call after they get drunk. One of the most simple and logical explanations said that alcohol lowers inhibition levels. A study said that the purpose of drunk calling could vary. It could be for social lubrication, entertainment, coordination, confession or perhaps to look for a partner or company for the night. Whatever the reason was, the point was clear—people tend to communicate and call each other when drunk.

I showed the articles to George. It took a bit of convincing for him to give it a try, but he did. We created history.

I had been at the company for a year or so and was getting more and more engrossed in how pricing could be optimized to increase sales through analytics. Out of all the product choices, I chose something that had always been a standard price—a popular beer stubby. I used to enjoy this delicacy in Australia at the Clarendon's in New Castle with Dean. We used to end our every meeting over there by mutually claiming in chorus "Beer is proof that God loves us and wants us to be happy." It's amusing that such words were originally said by an intellectual named Benjamin Franklin. When I approached the Business Manager, to set up a meeting, I was anticipating a positive response, but he seemed pretty cold. I had a series of successive triumphs with multiple products, and now, I expected quite the opposite I was completely confounded by his indifference. Crestfallen I still persisted, and got Charlie involved to make the meeting happen.

This Business Manager, Den, was in his sixties, had a pale, straight face. His personality reminded me of my class teacher in sixth grade back in India who I hated. I met him in his cabin and started the drill with the basic idea of my findings, but realized that he was not paying attention. He attended the meeting because senior management had asked him to.

"So, as I was saying, we need to change the pricing of our stubby. The current standard price is $36..." I paused for a bit to check whether he was still not paying attention and then went on, "I suggest we change the price to $37.50 for better sales." I had his attention before I could finish.

"So, you mean to say that I should increase the price of my product and it will sell more?" He asked, adjusting his round, golden-framed spectacles.

"Yes, that's what I suggest," I said smiling. He frowned and gave me a hopeless look. He removed his glasses and laid them on the neat glass table top.

"I don't think so. Please take your game of numbers somewhere else and destroy someone else's business, my beer stubby crate will be sold at the price it is at right now." He dismissed me and expected me to leave, but I was not there to give up.

"I know you have experience with the product, but the world is changing, and if we don't submit to change, we perish!" I gave him a bit of wisdom on change, but that, I think, made him more enraged.

"Who exactly hired you, boy? How old are you? 35? 40? I have been managing this product for more years than you have spent on Earth. Now do me a favour and please never bring such bizarre ideas in here again and waste my time," he said in a huff.

Den didn't know that I had done my homework before suggesting the price increase. That particular brand of beer Stubby was not a new product. It had been on the market for years and the price had witnessed a lot of fluctuations. The price range for a beer stubby crate had been between $35 to $40. In a situation where prices had been changing, it was not necessary that the sales of the product were highest, when the price was lowest. The relationship between sales and demand can be studied with a Price Elasticity Model.

The Price Elasticity of demand is defined by the ratio of percentage change in quantity demanded and the percentage of the change in price. If this ratio is negative, it means the quantity demanded would decrease with the increase in price, and vice versa. The coefficient in the case of beer stubby crate was indeed negative, and a natural reaction to same would be either to keep the cost the same, or to reduce it.

However, revenue and profits are two different things. While the revenue implies total money earned, profit is the difference between the cost price and selling price. Naturally, profit is more important than the revenue. In the case of the beer stubby crate, the profits earned on each product was much lesser because of the higher cost price. The price was to be increased and the revenue would go down, however, the profit of the company would increase because of higher margins. As there is a trade-off—too much decline in price will erode margins—too much rise will erode the demand. Thus, the objective was to find that perfect balance which will give optimal results.

By preparing a price elasticity model, we could figure out the maximum we can increase the price for higher profits at expense of lost revenues. I had a rough time explaining this to Den, for whom more sales implied more money.

My advice to Den was to increase the price by $0.26, as the price elasticity model predicted that it would increase the profit significantly as the number of customers who would buy the stubby crate will not decrease much, but profit will increase significantly.

And that's what happened. That week, the profit of beer stubby was highest in the last couple of years. Den liked the outcome so much he decided to use analytics for two more of his beer products.

With another success with Den, we were invited to be part of the solution of a major crisis the company faced. A new German company had entered the market and offered similar products to ours at lower prices. This new company had a reputation of entering new markets and destroying existing competitors at the roots. Our company was hit badly by the 15 new stores the other company established, especially since they mushroomed in no time. Customers were flooding to the new stores and their basket of products became divided. They bought a few products from us and a few from them— depending upon the price. The elasticity of the demand was having a negative impact on our company and this meant that pricing became the governing aspect of the company sale rather than goodwill.

Business Perspective

Management was worried because this wasn't some regular departmental problem, or an issue with one particular product line of the company; this was an attack on the whole company. Thus, Charlie and I found ourselves in a high-level meeting with the top management of the company.

"Charlie, can you do something?" The CEO of the company asked upfront. This guy was one of the unapproachable ones at the company. He didn't meet people easily. But such a question coming from him to Charlie was a victory in itself, and I was happy I had contributed to that. Going from almost being forced to leave through conditions orchestrated to be nearly impossible to survive, to being asked if he could save the company. Charlie had come a long way and I had been his companion and support.

"Only Shailendra can tell," Charlie said, sipping his tea with poise. They all looked at me. In such a short span, I had fallen in love with his pleasantly cynical attitude. His idea was to create space for wisdom and then state the obvious, making it sound like a miracle. I was a ghost to them. They had heard of me. They knew what I had done in the past, but they had never seen me or met me.

"I did some analysis before the meeting, but it is too early to say anything," I stated clearly.

"Is there hope?" The CEO asks, and I look at Charlie for a hint. I knew the solution, but needed Charlie's approval to say yes or no at the moment. That's where Charlie's role became important. I almost felt like Bonnie to the Clyde of the company, of course in a more civilized sense. How much to reveal, and when to reveal, is critical, and Charlie was the master at this. He nodded softly, in an unnoticeable way.

"Yes, there is…" I said …But I need time."

Even though it was a matter which couldn't wait, there were not many options. If we couldn't beat the competitor and send them back to Germany, we could help our company to keep its stake and hold in the market and not perish

Customer Perspective

This certainly was done by the help of follow-up data generated from the loyalty campaigns which showed us the massive lack of organisation in the localized markets. Being a FMCG and food processing organisation, the company was always focused in the macro market, while the micro dynamics of the market were regulated by the dealers and contractors to whom we supplied.

We could have marketed our hearts out, but in the end, the meat business doesn't come with many visible tags and identification when sold at local joints. Meat is mere flesh to people even if it is wrapped in our label. In the end, the store or outlet is what counts, or for that matter, the price, as was evident in our case. What we deciphered from the follow up on the campaigns was that the sales channels were not leading directly to the consumers. And in any case, if there hadn't been any provisions like loyalty points, they wouldn't have known about the company as much as Tim, the local beef vendor. We just weren't visible.

From our analysis, we found that we should let the competitor share our current market percentage while we focused on assessing the unorganized segment. Doing so would help us create a deeper connection with the consumers. This was expected to increase our direct sales and expand the market. Our calculations suggested that this way we would make the competitor appear like an outcast in our market and that would be our victory.

Solution

The competition's stores had been opening for more than a year, but they were never a major threat to the company. Hence, the company never heeded this hydra that was being nurtured in plain sight. But, when the market share percentage of this new company started soaring higher than what we could handle, we couldn't afford to avoid the situation any longer. We had to face it.

To discover the damage done to the company because of new stores being opened, the first step was to prepare a predictive model which would give us a list of customers that would be impacted. The second question was: by how much?

We had to do an analysis on all the stores that had opened in the last year in different localities and find the pattern of customer defection. Since the stores hadn't opened on the same day, the data couldn't be fed to the model. Hence, we had to realign the data while assuming that all stores opened the same day. The recalibration was done in a way that the final data set was obtained for the eight weeks before the store opened, and the eight-week period after the store opened. That was a huge task in itself, as we had to realign a huge database and also map the customers who regularly shop at those stores. It took us about three days just to process the data, but then everything was aligned and ready for modelling.

Another task was to define what a defected customer was. Some customers go over completely to the competition and some only do part of their shopping with the competition. Hence, it was important to define the objective and get everyone in the business on the same page.

We agreed the definition of the defective customer as someone who has dropped their spend by 20% week on week over 4 weeks in a row.

With this data, we developed two different models:

1. Customer Defection Probability

Once we agreed on the defection criteria, building the model was fairly simple. We built three predictive models and picked the best one with fair accuracy levels. The most accurate model was the regression model, which predicted the probability of customer defection in a particular locality if a new store was being opened there. The accuracy levels were pretty strong, as the model was 84% accurate.

2. Prediction of customer spend drop

This model predicted if the customer had started to spend less money in our store after a new store opened, and if so, how much. This model was developed with the help of two recently opened stores, and then it was tested. As the model was numerical, we tried a Random Forest and a CART Model. Again, we tested for the accuracy of both the models and found out the Random Forest was a more accurate model in this case. We could very easily and fairly accurately predict the amount by which each customer would be impacted by the opening of a competitor's new store.

With these two models, we were able to figure out which particular customers were at risk and might change the way they spend their money at our store, whenever a new competitor store opened in a particular area.

The dates on which a new competition store would open were known to us (thanks to their own marketing). So, we went ahead and scored each customer who lived in the vicinity of the competitor's new store. We then designed a personalised campaign for each customer to provide them with a better experience which resulted in not losing the customers to the competitors.. Saving your employer, and earning the respect that you gain after that, is one of the most satisfying things you can experience.

Business Perspective

The company survived and my thirst to explore more opportunities of incremental revenue through analytics reached new heights.

I had saved a product, ran a campaign, optimized the bundles and combos, averted the threat from a competitor. But one thing I had not done yet was to introduce new products that could take the company to new heights while gaining a stronger hold on the market. We had the customers, but we wanted to sell more things to them than they were already buying elsewhere.

I ran through the same loyalty program data to figure out our best-selling products, identify what people were likely to buy, and determine whether we already had those items in our store.

Customer Perspective

It was a fact that the customers didn't buy only from us. We all have our favourites. We had to become an omni-favourite. Customers were going to other stores for many other products. What we wanted to do was figure out where they are going and how much they were spending so we could predict a spend stretch and introduce the new products accordingly.

Until now, all we had done was use internal data and the behaviour of the customers which were regularly buying from us.

The objectives were to retain them, make them buy more, or simply ensure they stayed with us.

Finding out what they are doing outside our store was a major challenge which demanded some massive orbit changes in the company strategy. But we were unstoppable, and so are the possibilities of analytics. What we did next was something even bigger than what we had done before.

When the company said they wanted to introduce new products, there were innumerable options. Which of them would work best for the company? Again, the idea of this exercise was to make our customers buy more, rather than acquire new customers. In case new customers came because of the campaign, it would be nothing but the cherry on the top of our well-iced cake.

So, which were the products we didn't have that our customers were buying from the competition? There was no way to figure that out. But if we knew which store they are going to, and how much they are spending—this could pave the way to move ahead.

It was clear that this was essentially external data and no competitor would share their own data so we could utilise it to beat them. Charlie and I had been thinking about it, but we couldn't think of anything that would get us the data we needed. I realised I had been deviating from my own approach. I realised I was not thinking like a customer.

A customer buys certain products from us and then goes to another store to buy something else. There is one common point in these two processes–that is a transaction of money against goods. What if we become the enabler of this transaction and access the power to know the details of this transaction? What if the mechanism of this transaction becomes the source of data that we desperately need? It was a eureka moment—minus the fact that I was more ecstatic than Archimedes would have been.

I told this to Charlie and he set up a meeting in no time with the CEO himself. We had some reputation with him by now. Fast forward to the CEO's cabin.

"We have figured out the first new product that we need to launch," Charlie said.

"Isn't it too early? What is it?"

"A credit card," Charlie said with his face shining of happiness.

The CEO was confused. It was obvious that we had to explain to him how launching a credit card for our customers would allow us to monitor their purchasing behaviour outside the store. It was a smart way for data collection—a way which, at one point, looked extreme, but at another point, it looked simple and obvious. Had this been our first attempt of unlocking the power of analytics for growth, I swear he wouldn't have agreed. But he had seen how we saved the company and he was curious to see how we would get our users to buy even more from us.

A few months later we rolled out a credit card with special privileges for our customers. The credit card acted as a raven for us—scouting all across town and fetching us the data of how much was being spent where. Now, while this couldn't tell us exactly what our customers were buying, we could at least tell which other stores they were going to and how much they were spending. In short, the basket size at other stores was finally revealed.

This unlocked the opportunity to run more personalised campaigns and make our customers spend more money at our store. The credit card was a big success and a win-win deal. It was in itself a product and made money for the company while at the same time, providing data on customer purchasing behaviour at other stores.

We also launched two other products as testing models—mobile phones and pet insurance on the simple pretext that customers were already buying phone recharge and pet food from us. This made it more than obvious that they will need something more around those products, as well.

When I completed my term as an external consultant and it was time for me to say goodbye to the company, it was a moment to look back. I felt like I was standing at the top of a mountain and seeing the beautiful landscapes I had trod laid out around me. Every project we took up created incremental dollars for the company. I started working on a program in which no one believed. And that day, it was the most popular program in the country.

My retail experience has had a multi-level journey:

- Getting the sales up for a product with declining sales
- Making new combinations
- Price Optimization
- Surviving Competition
- Introducing New Products

Each of the above stated problems are unique in ots own way, as we kept changing methods and approaches to solve each one of them. We took creativity to its zenith and played with analytics to not only save the company, but take it to the next level as well.

"We did it," I said.

I could not thank Charlie enough for giving me an opportunity to generate incremental revenue of more than $250 million annually for the company. I learned a lot while working here. I earned experiences, patience, creativity, persistence and a zeal to never give up when you have the power of analytics in hand. In between all those numbers, a solution is always hiding. All you need is the eye and the drive to dig it out, and as Charlie always said: "Nothing Succeeds like Success."

Key Message/Myth Buster:

To make money out of data, you need more than just creative thinking. You also need an in-depth understanding of business. Understanding the customer journey and the impact on the customer experience is the key to the success of any analytics initiative. It is pivotal to know the business before you approach the business problem with any kind of idea.

-9-

Fundamental Principles

The case stories discussed earlier were full of challenges not specific to just those companies. Rather, organisations across the world continue to face similar challenges. Analytics is a field that finds unique and innovative solutions to problems, and continues to grow and evolve and help change the way business problems are looked at and solved.

The process is very similar to fighting a battle. Imagine a king waging war on a neighbouring kingdom, and he is on the verge of losing. Finally, he decides to send his special unit of warriors to save the battle. The preceding stories were about kings fighting losing battles. We will soon discover how this special unit of warriors fought the battle and saved the king.

But before that, it is imperative to learn what preparations the special unit made before going into battle. What is this special unit all about? There are so many stories and an aura of mystery around this unit. What is it, really? Why it is special, and what are its battling techniques? This special unit of warriors is analytics. Let's learn what analytics is before we learn how it saved those kings from losing their battles.

Difference between IT thinking and analytical thinking

As discussed before, it is a myth that analytics is an IT function. However, the reason why analytics goes beyond IT encompasses a treacherous journey with many twists and turns. Unfortunately, due to the fact that it involves coding, it seems as if analytics is part of the IT division in an organisation. This is one of the main reasons why organisations are not able to drive huge data value from analytics.

Before we explain the difference between IT and analytics, let's try and understand how IT works to determine its scope.

Approach and functioning of IT & Analytics

1. IT approach towards delivery of projects

Typically, an IT project involves installation of software and hardware using the right technology on time and to plan, and executing a given plan within a designated budget. IT projects are extremely sequential and consist of well-defined steps. In any corporation, the IT department asks for a business's requirement, and a business requirement document is filled out. The IT processes are then applied to code, or created in an environment that the business will use. When the delivery is done, the business does a user acceptance test and then adopts the model.

Generally, an IT project has the following steps:

1. Feasibility study/concept exploration
2. Concept of operations
3. System Requirements
4. High-Level Design
5. Detailed Design
6. Software/Hardware Development
7. Field Installation
8. Unit/Device testing
9. Subsystem verification
10. System Verification and Deployment
11. System Validation
12. Operations and maintenance
13. Changed and Upgrades

As you can see, over the years, we have been able to define very structured processes for IT with a lot of rigor around the steps so IT projects can be successfully delivered. The structured approach has now become the DNA of the IT Teams.

2. Analytics approach

The scope of analytics is completely different than the process involved with an IT project. So is the functioning. The scope of analytics is to solve a business problem or meet an objective in a creative way. The functioning of analytics is lucratively creative and demands an out of the box kind of approach to achieve the goals. We will learn more about functioning in the coming sections.

Analytics is an iterative process and requires business knowledge. In case business knowledge is not applied to analytics, the results obtained can be obvious and might fail to add any value.

3. Difference between IT and Analytics

It is clear that an IT project is well defined with several steps in fixed sequence to be executed one after the other. However, an analytics project can never be treated the same as traditional IT projects which have a designated outcome to be reached and a pre-planned process that needs to be followed. Analytics are used to get data so you can study your customers or a particular target group in order to understand the answers to various consumption patterns and problems. The data is also used to develop hypotheses and gain knowledge and understanding by conducting experiments—and eventually, to reach decision making that can fulfil the objectives of the business as discussed earlier.

In spite of the massive investment in this sector, there have been low returns on the use of analytics. Most of the investment in analytics is carried out through the acquisition of hardware and software, and very little of the organisation's investment funds are used to engage people who create value out of the environment. The reason for this is that analytics projects are treated the same way as every IT project since they are viewed in basically the same way

However, as stated earlier, there are differences between analytics and IT projects. Below are a few points which elaborate why the two fields are different, and why analytics should be treated differently.

Analytics can be unstructured and creative, and focuses on asking the right question

As discussed, IT is mundane and structured, and the project needs to stick with the designed path. But analytics, on the other hand, can be very unstructured in the statistical process adopted. Analytics is all about constant innovation and finding creative ways to achieve better results.

In analytics projects, it is important, and challenging, to ask the right questions. IT projects, on the other hand, just need to receive the designated outcome they have set for themselves.

For an analytics project, you need a dedicated team of professionals with an iterative approach to define and redefine questions to understand what works best for building the models, and how results can be validated in a short, iterative cycle.

People are at the heart of analytics projects

While IT is a very objectively-driven process, analytics is subjective, and needs to keep people at its centre. Though generating output is important, creating insights and recommendations from the output is key. So, the people who interpret results produced by the technology deployed, and those who execute the new decisions and directions, are at the heart of any analytics project.

Use of information to unlock value in analytics

Analytics projects use empirical evidence to assess a situation. A situation is understood with the help of mental models, experiences and essential knowledge from the data collected. An organisation's culture can play a significant role in how people make decisions, share information and how they collaborate. Traditional IT development ignores these factors completely. In IT projects, data which is identified as important, or can be controlled, is used. This approach is excellent when dealing with activities that are highly structured. It can be utilised successfully in systems and projects where the task is precisely described, such as processing customer orders.

If the data has to be converted into useful information while it is being taken from technological domain to human domain, IT processes fails.

Analytics need behavioural and statistical modellers which IT professionals are not

IT professionals are logical thinkers who fail to process data when it is related to human behaviour. Analytics projects require people versed in the statistical and behavioural sciences who understand the human mind well, understand how people perceive problems, and how they analyse data to form effective solutions and develop new ideas. Behavioural and cognitive scientists can use their knowledge in social psychology and cognitive sciences to predict how people behave in markets and economies. Many top organisations have already started to include behavioural scientists in the IT fields to carry out effective analytics.

IT responds to a requirement while analytics responds to an outcome

Analytic projects concentrate on finding business solutions while IT is about deploying technology to fulfil a requirement. Analytic projects try to find real-world solutions related to business rather than using technology to come up with a different system. Analytics help provide complex solutions related to how to advertise a product, how to interact with customers and what type of products to produce. Analytic data is used to understand social interaction and relationships. IT responds to pre-defined requirements, whilst analytics gets restricted if there is a pre-defined requirement.

The Plumbing

Plumbing is a common terminology used extensively in the field of IT. By plumbing, they mean laying down the path for variables and managing the connections from various data sources. It is popularly said that if the *Plumbing is right*, the system is going to yield the right answer.

Which means, if you set up the variables, data flow and the formulas, then you will always get a correct report every day until any part of the plumbing is broken. This is a typical IT process. You need to define the processes to get the right answer. Hence, it is completely process driven.

In the case of analytics, if the process is not broken, you will not be able to see the hidden patterns and possibilities in the data. So, it is important to break the plumbing, which is absolutely the opposite of a structured IT process.

You must break the pipe after the plumbing is done. By doing so, the variables from different data sources can interact with each other in multiple creative ways. This yield results which were otherwise not visible because of a fixed plumbing mechanism. The breaking of plumbing and the interaction of variables is then able to explain a number of relationships and correlations between variables which can identify flaws and improve business by improvising established processes or creating new ones.

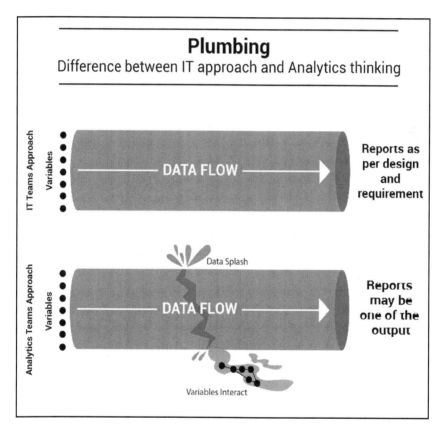

The key to the success of an analytics project is identifying the hidden patterns within the data to address the objective of the project. If you keep on doing what you are doing, you will keep on getting what you have been getting. Hence, if you have already defined the output, then you will get the same output and nothing new will be found.

Defining a requirement ahead of the process defeats the purpose of analytics. It draws a box around the thinking process and points it in one direction. So, when using analytics, there should be broad business problem statements initially to address rather than defining specific requirements. Remember, analytics is a business function; IT is just an enabler.

Assume there is a business problem in a corporation. The IT department wants the business to define the requirement so the necessary technology can be deployed and the infrastructure created to address the problem. But the business team is non-technical and they are simply unaware of what IT can do. Nor do they know what options are available with IT. While the business fails to define, and fails to ask, IT fails to deliver. Hence, the gap is observed. Even though, the business is aware of the problem they are facing, still the analytics solution is unable to help them.

Let us take a different view. What if the problem is not defined? This requires an altogether different approach. In order to identify hidden patterns within the data, the above approach usually does not work. Instead to asking a question and trying to solve it, we need an approach where we want the data to help ask the question. Imagine, you are on a beach, you take the sand into both your hands, shake the hands and then throw the sand on the beach to see that the sand self-aligns itself in a pattern that shows some insights that you can take action on.

With a huge analytical advancement in technology over the past few years, machine learning techniques can troll into large value and identify hidden behavioral patterns which are not known to naked eye. Pattern recognition requires advanced automation of analytical techniques where the models are self-learning and recalibrate in real time based on the changing data. Thus, coming out with an outline of insight that was never known to business in the past.

Analytics is creativity within the business world. The analytics team should possess the business knowledge, statistical ability and data knowledge. They define the business problem, discover the right question to ask, and accordingly, a business requirement document can be completed. IT develops the infrastructure that enables the analytical data to be extracted to answer the question.

However, because of half-baked knowledge, ignorance and businesses being unaware of how analytics should function— companies are not able to exploit analytics in a manner that will help their business grow. Analytics is being confused with IT, and IT professionals are being assigned the tasks of analytics.

Just remember, analytics is about possibilities and probabilities and providing answers to business questions that positively impact the decision-making process in relation to diverse business problems. IT is about building infrastructure and getting outputs in alignment with a preconceived direction.

There are things, we know we don't know and there are things we don't know, we don't know. Pattern recognition helps in finding things we don't know, we don't know.

Analytics Sophistication and its components

Different people have different perspectives about analytics, maybe because there are many different tiers within the scope of analytics. Some people refer to simple data crunching as analytics, while some refer to filing reports as analytics. To say these things are not part of data analytics would not do the field, or the people, justice. Finally, it is more appropriate to say different organisations use different levels, or layers of analytics, and some of these layers are more sophisticated than others.

As mentioned, analytics works in tiers, and there are levels of sophistication. In fact, analytics does not translate to one single linear process. Rather, it is a misrepresented term with multiple processes that move in and out of the different tiers or levels within the field. Different organisations manage their businesses at these different tiers of analytics. These tiers can be listed as:

- Managing Information / Data Management
- Descriptive Analytics
- Predictive Analytics
- Prescriptive Analytics

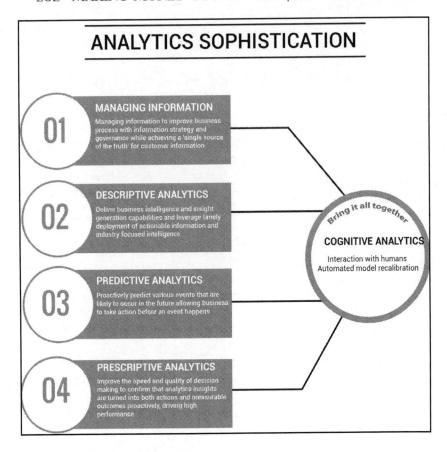

ANALYTICS SOPHISTICATION

01 MANAGING INFORMATION
Managing information to improve business process with information strategy and governance while achieving a 'single source of the truth' for customer information

02 DESCRIPTIVE ANALYTICS
Deliver business intelligence and insight generation capabilities and leverage timely deployment of actionable information and industry focused intelligence

03 PREDICTIVE ANALYTICS
Proactively predict various events that are likely to occur in the future allowing business to take action before an event happens

04 PRESCRIPTIVE ANALYTICS
Improve the speed and quality of decision making to confirm that analytics insights are turned into both actions and measurable outcomes proactively, driving high performance

Bring it all together
COGNITIVE ANALYTICS
Interaction with humans
Automated model recalibration

Analytics, as a holistic process, consists of all these tiers. However, one of the important aspects that are most commonly confused about analytics is the fact that the sequence of these components is not a mandate to be always followed. Since analytics is usually put into the IT division, which has an inherent tendency to do things sequentially, IT ends up applying sequential processes to analytics and the return on investment is drastically impacted with longer project cycles than required.

In analytics, the sequences in which each process is written is not a hard and fast rule, and it is not a sin to not start from step 1. On the contrary, a little creativity is appreciated to break the monotony by trying something new in the way of an experiment. The sequence can be very well followed; but, as emphasized before, analytics helps understand the business problem by finding the right questions. Hence, the first step might not be managing information. It might be some predictive analysis. This way, higher Return on Investment can be achieved early in the lifecycle of the project and can highlight what type of data to store first.

Data Management

If we imagine analytics as a basic manufacturing process, data would perhaps be the raw material. Just like in any other manufacturing or industrial process, the following attributes related to the raw material are extremely important:

- Quality of raw material (in this case relevance)
- Consistent supply of raw material
- Proper flow of raw material
- Pipeline and linkages for raw material for proper flow

We can also imagine that data is like the life blood of an organism. And just like different organisms can have different blood groups, different types of data sets are needed for different kinds of business problems. At the same time, the flow of blood with the right pressure is important for the organism to function properly. The same goes for data.

Data management has several components and steps in an analytics perspective:

1. Identifying data sources and creating a plan

The probable data sources are identified, and a plan is made as to how this data will be stored, and how groups of data could be linked to each other when required.

2. Storage of data at one single place

It is important to store data from multiple sources to one single place from where different people can access it. Typically, a business will run into problems if they attempt to store data in multiple locations and have various people accessing it from different sources. Hence, storing data at one single place becomes critically important so as to get the single source of the truth.

3. Accessibility of Data

While the data is stored, it is important that the data is available and accessible to different stakeholders whenever and wherever they want. Easy accessibility speeds up the entire process and makes it smoother.

4. Data Quality Management

The quality of data is to be assessed, and it is ensured that the data is consistent and in the right granularity needed. The data needs to be clean and standardised in the platform as it is coming from multiple sources and may vary in consistency.

5. Data Security

Unsolicited manipulation or stealing of data can be hazardous for the company and hence data security is one of the key points of data management.

Sometimes, the above four components are addressed through a data warehousing management company. Bill Inmon, who is known as the father of data warehousing, defines it as:

A data warehouse is a subject-oriented, integrated, time-variant and non-volatile collection of data in support of management's decision-making process.

Data warehousing is mostly kept separated from the operational databases of the company, and once the data is stored, it is not changed. Hence this is the historical data which can be used for analytics.

The data management tier addresses one or all of the above four components and aims to become a single version of truth for all stakeholders. It collects the data coming in from different sources on a regular basis and stores it in a way that is readily accessible.

2. Descriptive Analysis

This tier is comprised of describing or summarizing raw data to present it in a simple, accessible format. The data is very critical information that allows the reader to learn from past behaviours since it gives an idea of 'what has happened'. Such deeds can be rectified to improve upon future outcomes.

Descriptive analysis employs data aggregation to probe into the past and tell what has been done. The typical descriptive analysis is usually characterized by:

- Traditional reporting
- Slicing/Dicing of data through Business Intelligence
- Data Visualisation
- Dashboarding

TRADITIONAL REPORTING - The whole drive behind descriptive analysis is not just to understand the past and summarize it in a comprehensible form, but also to make sure that the same data, information, or perhaps the outcome, is available at the right time and as needed. Hence, the timely generation of insights and industry focused reports is the key objective of this kind of analysis.

SLICING/DICING - In layman's terms, descriptive analysis basically describes the data in a form that can be interpreted by the human mind. It does this through a slice and dice approach on the data so that more information can be yielded.

DATA VISUALISATION - Recently, data visualisation tools that can visualize various aspects of data on graphs, maps, pictures and more have become very popular. It is difficult to look at data in spreadsheets. People are usually stuck while gazing at the static numbers in the cells which don't communicate the real story behind these numbers.

DASHBOARDING - Data visualisation tools let you visualise data on simple and easy-to-use platforms called dashboards. Not only that, but the dashboard has the ability to connect directly with the data so it is feeding the critical metrics with real-time information.

These tools help you keep all your metrics in one place and keep them clear, relevant and updated. At the same time, these tools offer you the flexibility to reassemble, reorganise and change the visualisation in any particular way you wish. The changes in data can be seen in real time and can help in assessing the outcome of various actions instantaneously.

Furthermore, once it is ascertained which visuals and reports are to be monitored on a regular basis by an organisation's leadership, they are converted into dashboards to monitor various Key Performance Indicators.

Inferences and insights are drawn purely from the summarisation of data. The data tells you what happened. It highlights some focus areas that you might have overlooked and helps you understand the pain points. However, it does not tell you why you have the problem, how it happened, or how you can avoid it in the future or make it happen again if you want to.

3. Predictive Analysis

Predictive analysis is one of the critical products of said basket. It is the process of predicting the events and situations of an unknown future.

By executing predictive modelling analysis tests that validate and evaluate data, predictions can be made about what is going to happen in the context of a particular business scenario which is helpful in a number of ways. Predictive modelling is done by learning the reasons why something happened in the past, and then applying that knowledge to know what is going to happen in the future.

These days, with growing rivalry, enterprises can benefit from predictive analysis to increase their productivity and hence increase competitive advantage. Predictive analytics is widely used in almost all functions within an organisation to both increase revenue and optimise processes to reduce costs. Some very common uses of predictive analysis are:

- Churn Analysis
- Propensity to buy

- Fraud Detection
- Network optimisation

4. Prescriptive Analysis

Prescriptive analytics takes analysis to the next higher level. While predictive analysis may know the reason why something happened, it can't suggest what must be done to obtain better results. Here, prescriptive analysis is a step ahead. In this type of, analytics, the data takes the user beyond knowing what is going to happen, and when, into also understanding the reason behind it. When this future event is unveiled, it can be used as an opportunity for the organisation. Prescriptive analytics studies the data around an event and is then able to suggest what can be done to obtain better results. This type of analysis reveals the implications of every possible option in the decision-making process and can also mitigate possible future risks.

Prescriptive analysis has the ability to continuously take new data, re-predict and re-prescribe on its own. Hence, the prediction accuracy is improvised and the decision making becomes more accurate. This type of analysis has the ability to absorb hybrid data—that is the structured and unstructured data, along with the business' rules to prescribe how to make maximum use out of future events.

Prescriptive analytics is evidently complex and not easy to administer. However, if it is implemented with perfection, the decision-making process of a business can be hugely and positively impacted. Prescriptive analytics is now being used successfully for the optimisation of production, scheduling and inventory management in the supply chain—which ensures that the right products are being delivered at the right time, and the customer experience is being optimised.

Next Generation: Cognitive - Bringing all the above together (Artificial Intelligence)

Cognitive analytics brings all these tiers together in a self-learning and self-calibrating environment while making use of machine learning, but providing the final outcome in forms of regular human interactions.

The term cognitive technology refers to how a machine can facilitate interaction with humans while using structured or unstructured data. This process also consists of the application of self-learning/machine learning models for predicting outcomes in advance.

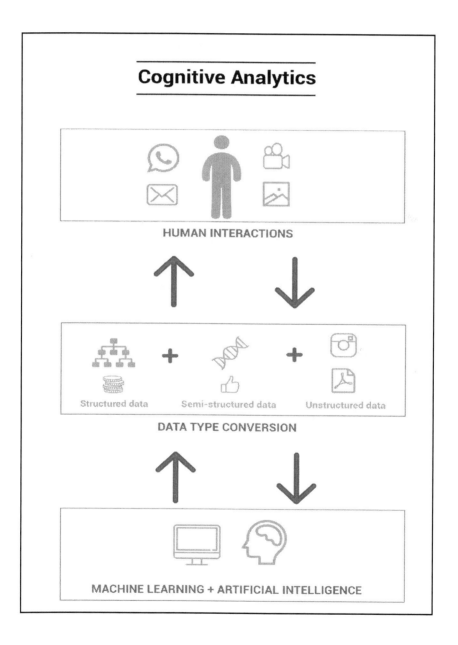

Steps for cognitive computing:
1. Ingestion of information

The information is ingested from a variety of forms: textual, audio, video or visual. The input data can be structured, semi-structured or unstructured, or maybe even a random mix of these. Itis then absorbed to be processed further.

2. Interpretation of information

The information is interpreted through processes like Natural Language Processing (for audio) and Deep Learning (for videos and pictures).

Natural Language Processing (NLP)

NLP applications let humans speak to the computer. Human speech is not precise and there are uncountable variations to it. There are different dialects, languages and many other complex variables, and hence, requires a medium through which speech can be interpreted by the computer. It performs sentence segmentation, speech tagging and parsing (analysing it in an orderly way to understand relationships and meanings). The application performs deep analysis and named entity extraction—which means identifying one item from bigger data sets and attributing it to the input received. This is how data is interpreted by the computer through deep learning.

Deep Learning

In the previous step (natural language processing), we learned how text and audio are ingested and processed by the system. Deep Learning is the process through which images and videos can be interpreted by the system. Deep Learning uses Artificial Neural Networks (ANN) to process data. These networks are highly interconnected data processing elements very much like our biological neurons.

The basic idea is this: for a computer, an image is a grid of multiple pixels. The darkness of the pixel is represented by a number. Hence, when the ANN network is fed pictures, it sees and processes a grid of numbers which is actually a representation of a picture. Similarly, a video is a series of pictures which can be further broken down to pixels and numbers. This is how deep learning interprets images and videos.

Accessing other data sources

Once the data is interpreted by the computer, it needs to be processed. While the computer might already have a lot of internal data, there is always the need of external data sources. With the help of the internet, this external data is fetched. Depending upon the problem statement, the data can be anything from weather data to knowledge about what is happening in the world.

Learning Base Machine Models

With the help of initial data, the system starts to learn the base machine-learning models. This is the first step of learning, and first rules will be made here which are entirely based on what the system knows already.

Recalibration of model

This is the intelligent aspect of the model. It is here that the model becomes cognitive and enters the arena of artificial intelligence. Now, as more and more data is ingested through responses, the model keeps on self-learning and recalibrating itself to provide ever more precise results. This is a continuous iterative process, and every time the answers become more intelligent.

Responds back to user in the same way using various devices

After calibration and processing, the final answer is generated. However, this answer is given back to the user exactly in the same form the input was received. For example, if the input was an audio, the answer can be given back in audio by using the same interpretation techniques as were used for inputs.

The machines are now intelligent enough to ingest any kind of data and do any tier of analytics to provide the required outcome.

There are robots available that can work proficiently in place of humans by using cognitive analytics. Imagine an interaction between a human and a robot working as a concierge at a hotel.

You go to the hotel and ask the robot,

"Good evening! Can I get a cab?"

The robot takes this voice data and processes it. This input which is in form of voice can also be in the form of a text or a visual. The information is ingested and the robot provides you an output:

"Good evening, Ma'am! Where to?"

The voice input helps the robot understand that the gender of the person is female, and a salutation is added accordingly. The greeting *'Good evening'* is responded back with a similar greeting. By applying predictive and prescriptive analytics over the information ingested, and by also using the past, stored data, the final action is generated in which the robot asks the human, 'Where to?' so that the next step can be taken. This action is presented to the human in the same way the input was provided, that is, in the voice format, since it is understood that the input source is competent with the same form of data.

Computers are not just learning through the inputs provided by humans. Instead, computers are also learning from their own mistakes and making a more *intelligent* and *informed* decision accordingly. While the possibility of computers building an autonomous network seems far-fetched, and the efficiency of the functionality of the same is largely debated, it is widely accepted that computers and humans are supposed to work together. Computers need to learn to interact with humans in a more intelligent way, which is exactly where the world of cognitive analytics is heading.

What we can expect in upcoming years is that humans and computers will be working directly together. This partnership will help achieve the best results in terms of speed, productivity and quality from machines with the emotional intelligence aspect provided by humans.

Analytics Delivery Process

The first step in the analytics delivery process is to define the business problem in plain English. The approach follows an analytical engagement process—with a clear focus on achieving high levels of data and insights quality through targeted and progressive stakeholder engagement. Defining the business problem in simple English is important, since everything that follows is dependent on that step of the process.

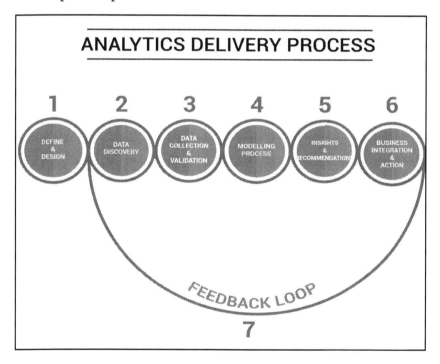

ANALYTICS DELIVERY PROCESS

1	2	3	4	5	6
DEFINE & DESIGN	DATA DISCOVERY	DATA COLLECTION & VALIDATION	MODELLING PROCESS	INSIGHTS & RECOMMENDATIONS	BUSINESS INTEGRATION & ACTION

FEEDBACK LOOP

7

Define and Design

Define and Agree on the Business Problem / Objective of the project

Defining the problem is perhaps the easiest, and in its own way, is a critical step. Data has a sly nature and can be deceptive in appearance. Often, when analysts are confused about the right statistical method to use, the real problem is that they haven't defined the right objective based on the business problem. They have a general idea of the relationship they want to test, but their idea is vague. The curious need to be specific for each objective must be written down in both theoretical and operational terms. The point here is to have the mathematical representation of the question at hand— we're dealing with data after all. This needs to be agreed upon with the business stakeholders since this is the critical success factor for the project.

Data Discovery

Data discovery is the process of identifying the data required to solve the business problem defined in the first step, and checking to see if that data is available. Multiple activities are undertaken in this phase.

1. Steps for Data Discovery

- A comprehensive dialogue with the key stakeholders is performed to understand the valuable data sets required for the problem.

- Check the availability and quality of data.

- After the key data points are identified and determined accessible, choose the variables and level of measurement to be implemented in answering the business problem.

- Every model must take into account both the design of the variables set and the level of measurement of those variables.

- Mind it, that level of measurement, is whether a variable is nominal, ordinal, or interval needs to be defined in this step. It's necessary to keep in mind if the Level of Measurement is determined after making continuous observations of a line of questioning or distributed accounts of random observations for identifying the homogeneity and synchronisation between variables.

- It's absolutely vital that you know the level of measurement of each response and predictor variable, because they determine both the type of information you can get from your model, as well as the family of models that is appropriate.

- An analysis plan is then written keeping in mind all the aspects of the business problem, data accessibility and data creation, if needed.

- The best guess for the statistical method is written that will answer the business problem question, taking into account the problem and the types of available data.

- The analysis method does not have to be final, it just needs to be a reasonable approximation. Basically, like taking the first baby step before getting into real brainstorming.

- New data points are created that are to be incorporated after a discussion with the business teams, stakeholders and the IT Teams.

- This is the point at which you should calculate your sample sizes before you collate data and after you have an analysis plan. You need to know which statistical tests you will use as a basis for the estimates.

- There really is no point in running post-hoc power analyses–it doesn't tell you anything. It's a fool's errand that basically returns to the premise that it starts with regarding the statistical significance based on true variance of samples and test method.

- To validate if the business problem is right or not, it is critical to be sure about the problem before starting the journey to seek answers to get insights that can add value.

- In case the business problem is not right, return to the first step and redefine it.

Output:

1. Validation of the stakeholders on the business problem, data and other key points.

2. An agreement on the analysis plan.

3. Ensuring that the data is available, accessible and ready.

4. Enabling the possibility of transfer of data.

The most important aspect of this stage is to engage with key business stakeholders to understand how they use data.

2 Infrastructure Setup

After the steps above are taken, it is of paramount importance to check whether there is the required infrastructure to process the data that has been discovered and will be collected in the coming steps.

The infrastructure has two prime components:

1. Hardware

When it comes to hardware for analytics, there are essentially two options for infrastructure:

- **On Premise** - When the entire infrastructure is in the same building and demands support and maintenance.

- **On Cloud** - When the infrastructure is not in same building and can be accessed remotely

There is a never-ending debate on deciding which of the two above options are better for storing the data and for analytics. However, again, it is not black and white. There are multiple factors influencing the decision, and the final choice depends on the situation, the kind of industry being analysed, and other factors. Here is a comparison for the on-premise and cloud-based infrastructure as per the attributes influencing them:

Factor	Preferred Solution	Reason
Government Regulations, Data Privacy and Security	On Premise	Some data is extremely sensitive, and there are strict government regulations around data privacy. In some cases, some data types are not even allowed to leave the shores of the country. Hence, it is preferred that the data is stored in private data centers.
Agility and Time	Cloud	The cloud environment facilitates a better scope for collaboration between partners as well as providing for easy implementation by transcending geographical boundaries. Therefore, the entire process become agile, saving valuable time for the organisation.
Degree of Customization	On Premise	For degree of customization for existing infrastructure, on premise is easier to work with when compared to cloud-based infrastructure.
Scalability and Cost	Cloud	In most cases, when the scale of the project is bigger, infrastructure is more costly. Using the cloud environment helps make the process more economical. The upfront investment for on premise is high, with additional IT costs. More than that, there are many unpredictable costs that the organisations must keep in mind.

2. Software

Software like The SAS Software, IBM's SPSS, Python and R Statistical Package (Commonly referred as R) enables the analytics. SAS encompasses the entire range of statistical analysis and techniques. On the other hand, R is an open source equivalent of SAS and there is an option for people to submit their own packages.

When compared to the traditional computing software like that of Excel and others, these software mentioned provides an edge while doing analytics:

- They can process large volumes and complex data with better agility
- Iteration is facilitated better
- Data exploration and sophisticated analysis is enabled
- Data from multiple SQL queries can be handled easily
- Matrix operations, linear algebra, differential equations and many other advanced mathematical operations can be done swiftly
- They have the ability to multi-plot while using various loops and functions
- User-defined functions can be used

Hence, analytics software is designed specifically to deal with complex statistical problems which also enable better processing and presentation of data in helping to solve a business problem as a whole.

Output: Ensuring that the infrastructure is ready to be used.

3. Data Collection and Validation
Types of Data

Data is a broad term and there are various kind of data which are now available. Speaking from an analytics perspective, data can be categorically divided into three segments:

1. Structured Data

Structured data is data that has been organized into a formatted repository, typically a database, so that its elements can be made addressable for more effective processing and analysis. It has a very organised format, strict data model and can be easily accessible through various queries and algorithms. Earlier, it was the only data form which could be stored, studied, and analysed because of low storage capacities and slow processing abilities. However, advanced technology made it possible to study other kinds of data as well.

Why is it called Structured?

It is called structured data because it can be classified within a database which is structured in simple rows (Records) and columns (Fields) and is stored in table format with the ability to link data from rows and columns together. It is the simplest form of data.

Examples of Structured Data are:

- Relational Databases
- Relational Tables
- Spreadsheets
- Delimited files

2. Semi-Structured Data

Semi-structured data is a form of data which has not been assigned into any particular database with specific functions but has some associated information which makes it easier to work on and analyse. The sources of this data have an almost defined structure, and the nature of this data is mostly textual. Semi-structured data lacks a strict data model. However, this data must be mined using different techniques so that the structured data can be further enriched.

Why is it called Semi-Structured?

Semi-structured lies somewhere between structured and unstructured data. Semi-structured data does not have fully classified values as is the case with structured data, but it has some information attached to it which makes it easier to classify when compared to unstructured data. The semi-structured data has some kind of a structure to it but it also contains free-flowing information within that structure.

Examples of Semi-Structured Data are:

- Social Media Feeds
- Email Conversations
- Electronic data interchange (EDI)

3. Unstructured Data

What is Unstructured Data?

Unstructured data is a form of unspecified data which does not have a pre-defined data structure and can't be organized in a pre-defined manner. These are the data sources that have no structure at all. This data doesn't have any well-defined or consistent fields and it is highly probable that it does not even contain any numbers and texts. This is the real gold mine. For any business, 80-90 percent of data is in the form of unstructured data.

Why is it called unstructured?

Unstructured data is highly cluttered, and at first, does not appear to make any sense. It requires great skill and proficiency to make sense of unstructured data. It is a collection of data from myriad sources clubbed together. In most cases, data collection is automatic and does not require human intervention.

Examples of unstructured data are:

- Voice Data: human voice data collected through phone calls, conversations, etc.

- Image Data: facial images, landscape images, x-ray images, etc.

- Videos Data: video content generated during events and other regular CCTV footage.

- Machine Data: data generated through cars, ships, mobile phones and other machines.

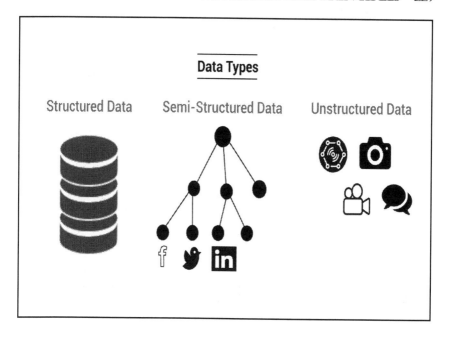

Analytics Dataset

After the data discovery has been done and the necessary infrastructure is in place, the data collection process is started and data from different sources (Internal and external) is transferred to one single source. The data is then collated into one large analytical dataset containing all data points. After bringing all data points together, various data processes are performed:

Data Quality Assessment

Assessment approach for data quality is:

- Decide what data items you will be using to check the data quality. Basically, it will be the data that is going to be critical for business operations and management reporting.

- Check which of the data quality dimension will be used and also define the associated weighting.
- Define the range of bad and good quality data. One data set can support more than one requirement, so different data quality assessments are performed.
- Assessment criteria should be applied to data items.
- Determine and review the end results to check the quality.

The six core dimensions of data quality are:

- Completeness
- Uniqueness
- Timeliness
- Validity
- Accuracy
- Consistency

Data Cleansing

Data cleaning means making the data consistent and filling in the missing gaps between the data so that it becomes suitable to be fed to the model.

Creating new variables

This step can be quite time-consuming. It's pretty rare for every variable needed for analysis to have been collected in exactly the right form. Thus, we create indices, categorize and reverse code to get variables in their final form, including running principal components or factor analysis.

Techniques also include creating dummy variables to assist in comparing various models. A trade secret also lies in offering a form of an equation to one latent variable and replacing it with a group of otherwise filtered out 'observed variables' from the data design stage.

Such techniques make data more rich and usable.

Run Univariate and Bivariate Statistics

You need to know what you're working with. Check the distribution trends of the variables you intend to use, as well as bivariate relationships among all variables that might serve the model.

Doing this, you may find something that leads you back to changing the data variables, or for that matter, changing the analysis plan altogether. You might have to do some data manipulation or deal with missing data.

More importantly, this level gives you a glimpse of some data based irregularities that may come up later in the analysis. But the sooner we know the sin, the sooner it can be absolved. Even if you don't discover the issue until later, at least the effort put into discovering irregularities in this stage may help prevent you from being thrown into a loop later if you have a good understanding of your variables.

Data Validation

The process of data validation means confirming and getting a sign-off from the stakeholders that the data is right in the context of size, quality and other parameters, and that the data is ready for modelling. Involve business teams and top-level management for the validation process.

Outcome: The validated data which is right, accessible and ready to be used.

4. Modelling Processes

A model, as the term implies, is an attempt to mimic reality. In statistics, it usually concludes to a mathematical equation that links the inputs to the outputs. The objective of 'modelling processes' is to find the model which will mimic this reality more often than not.

For modelling, we test the various combinations of input variables provided to find out and separate those variables which, in particular, have the capability to explain the problem. The best model is then selected by using statistical diagnostics and determining how accurate it is.

Statistical modelling is a very iterative process and needs to be done after the objective of the analysis is well defined. It is usually advised to start with small data sets and then increase the data sets for finer accuracy.

There are various types of statistical modelling techniques that are being utilized, some of them are categorized as follows:

LEARNING TYPE	MODEL TYPE	NAME	DESCRIPTION
Supervised Learning	Classification	Naïve Bayes	Simple probabilistic classifiers with strong independence assumptions between the features
		Nearest Neighbor	Classifies based on finding the point in a given set that is closest (or most similar) to a given point
		Discriminant Analysis	Finds a linear combination of features that characterizes or separates two or more classes of objects or events
	Regression	Linear Regression	Creates the best fit through all the data points
		Logistic Regression	Usually solves the Yes/No problems using a linear approach
		Decision Trees	Branching Method to identify all possible outcomes to a decision
		Random Forest	Combines multiple decision trees to get a better overall performance
		Gradient Boosting	Builds the model as stage-wise boosting, and then generalizes by allowing for optimization
		Neural Networks	Interconnected neurons passes message through layers
Unsupervised Learning	Clustering	K-Means	Partitions and clusters observations with the nearest mean
		Hierarchical	Builds a hierarchy and presents in a dendogram
		Gaussian Mixture	Probability distribution of continuous measurements or features
		Hidden Markov Model	Presented as the dynamic Bayesian Network where Only the output state is visible

The usual steps involved in a modelling process are:

a. Run an initial model

Once you know what you're working with, apply the model listed in your analysis plan. In all likelihood, this will not be the final model.

But, if most of the process has been followed correctly, this initial model should fall in the right ballpark of what you are looking for, and be able to work with the kind of variables and they type of design that will provide the answers to the business problem objective. This is the model that one keeps to build upon in order to reach the desired model.

b. Refine predictors and check model fit

If the object is a truly exploratory analysis, or if the point of the model is found to be purely predictive, you can always use some sort of stepped approach to determine the best predictors.

If the analysis is to test hypotheses or answer theoretical questions, this part will be more about refinement. You can test, and possibly drop, interactions and quadratic relations or explore other types of nonlinearity.

Drop non-significant control variables.Some of them might have been forcibly induced by yourself while designing and refining the data.

Check for greater variability than expected.

c. Test assumptions

Because you already investigated the right family of models in the first step by defining the mathematical form of the problem in a statement that addresses both logical and operational/philosophical sides of the issue, now you are ready to thoroughly investigate your variables by statistical analysis. Since you have also already correctly specified your model by setting legitimate predictors, there should be no big surprises here. Rather, this step will be about confirming, checking, and refining. But what you learn here can send you back to any of those steps for further refinement.

d. Check for and resolve data issues

The steps of assumptions checking and issue resolution are often done together, or perhaps a repeating cycle of one, and then the other. This is where you check for data issues that can affect the model, but are not exactly assumptions. These include:

Data issues which are about the data, not the model, but occur within the context of the model

- Multicollinearity
- Outliers and influential points
- Missing data
- Truncation and censoring

Once again, data issues don't appear until you have chosen variables and put them in the model.

e. Interpret Results

Now, finally, the time comes to start reaping what you've sown.

You may not notice data issues or specified predictors until you interpret the coefficients. Then you find something like a super-high standard error or a coefficient with a sign opposite what you expected, sending you back to previous steps.

If the model outputs are not accurate enough, or do not solve for the business problem / objective, then it may mean you need to iterate once again and make changes to either the input data or model until the model is strong enough and solves the business problem.

Output:

- The model itself
- Strength of the model, i.e. the accuracy levels
- Identification of lead indicators, predictors

Statistical modelling is not one single process but can employ multiple processes depending on the situation, objective and the problem statement.

5. Insights Generation and Recommendation

This is one of the most important steps in the analytics process. Many projects do not incorporate this step, and failure to implement it typically means failure of the analytics project. Insights are one of the key parts of the analytics process. They not only explain the outcome of models; they explain why the issue is occurring. While modelling is all about numbers and algorithms, insights are to be presented in a format that can be easily understood by the decision makers of the business.

Insights are basically actionable recommendations that are made to solve the business problem. They can be presented in form of a PowerPoint, graph, visuals or a simple text report. The insights and recommendations are supposed to be consumed by business professionals and hence should be in plain English in order to be easily understood.

6. Business Integration

It is usually said that a very good model is worth nothing if it is not executed. The model will only be executed if the business team has confidence in the output and if they are willing to execute; which can only happen if the business team understands the output.

The entire analytical process, logics used and insights generated—all of it has to be explained to the business executives involved in order for them to agree to execute. For business execution to occur, the analytics team needs to walk the business team through to the entire process and convince them, with the power of logic and models, to absorb the insights and embed analytics into their business process in order to solve their business problems.

If the insights reports are not integrated with the business, the whole exercise of the analytics is wasted. Even if business integration appears to be the last step, it has to be taken care of from the beginning. For every step you take in analytics, you must keep the business teams and the management involved and keep them in the loop on what you are doing, and why are you doing so.

If business integration is kept in mind from the beginning, the last step becomes easier since the business knows what you have been doing. Otherwise, it might be difficult to reason against the experience of management who are many times, rigid with what they know.

7. Feedback Loop

The model needs to learn from the results of the actions. Hence, there is a great need for getting the response of the actions/ results back into the model. This allows for effective monitoring and measuring of the output. The output of the model is checked for accuracy and quality of the model. The feedback from this check is sent back to the data discovery step where tweaks are made to improvise on the accuracy and consistency of the model. This is an iterative process until the accuracy of models are improved to the satisfaction of all involved.

Strategy

Unfortunately, lots of organisations have only used analytics at a tactical level. They encounter a business problem and then try to find solutions for those problems, tactically. It seems analytics functions is undermined and not taken as seriously as one would imagine though the expectations are quiet high. A strategic initiative is required by organisations in order to reap benefits from analytics, quickly.

Successful companies have a strategic intent around analytics. It gets leadership around the analytics function, who then designs, owns and delivers three roadmaps which have dependency on each other:

- **Business Analytics Roadmap:** This will showcase all the analytics functionalities that will be delivered to the business over a period of time.
- **IT Roadmap:** Infrastructure required to support the roll-out of the analytics functionalities and models
- **Customer Roadmap:** The positive impact on customer experience due to the implementation of the analytics functionalities.

All these three roadmaps need to have the blessing of the board and to deliver the overall strategy, Chief Analytics Officer is a must.

Chief Analytics Officer

It is very encouraging to see how organisations are increasing their investments on analytics as they acknowledge its rising importance (these budgets can go up to millions each year). This means that expectations for good and quick returns increase. With this, the challenge of no returns arises. Businesses often blame the function itself and are quick to conclude that analytics is a 'buzzword' that is not delivering real value. What they fail to see is that the fundamental problem is not the function of analytics. Rather, it is hiring the right people to deliver real value through the process of analytics. This then, no doubt, leads to a significant decline in investments for analytics if an organisation does not start reaping benefits and begin to witness its value.

Hence it is all about hiring the right talent for the right role and it always starts from the top. The Chief Analytics Officer plays an important role in all of this, not only for the analytics function, but also towards the entire investment on data and analytics.

1. Objective of the role

A Chief Analytics Officer has a strong command of the overall business goals and combines an overarching economic perspective with statistical expertise, proficiency in computer sciences and a raging passion for data-driven decision making. CAO sees business as a whole and aims for an optimum balance among operational metrics. The contribution of a CAO must be accounted for by Return on Investment and actionable insights along with an observed improvement in operations.

On the whole, the role of a CAO is to make money out of data. The most important role of the Chief Analytics Officer is to demonstrate and show value and succeed in taking the lead on an analytics journey. In organisations where a Chief Analytics Officer is able to demonstrate value, analytics functions are successful and they are no longer a cost centre, they are a profit centre. The Chief Analytics Officer is usually a storyteller who understands the art and science of analytics and showcases the value created through the work done by the team.

2. Skill-sets required for the role

- Good understanding of advanced analytics can be used to capitalize on data to make logical decisions which will yield better outcomes.
- Understanding of various analytics tools and hands-on experience to be able to showcase the art of possibility.
- Identifies right talent that will successfully deliver analytics projects and quickly drive value.
- Understanding of flow of information and its context. Moreover, its relevance across the enterprise.
- Great presentation and storytelling skills.

- Since analytics is a creative process, he must be a creative, innovative and out-of-the-box thinker who can bring new ideas in order to make money out of data.

3. Role and Responsibilities

- A CAO is the conduit between IT and business: helps business understand what to ask, and helps IT understand what to give.
- Is responsible for driving incremental revenue and optimise costs.
- Drives analytical thinking across the leadership by showcasing the art of possibility.
- Creates data and analytics products that can be monetised.
- Acts as a change catalyst: drives change in the business through analytics.
- Helps bring the analytics thinking into the business value chain.

The role of CAO is often confused with the role of CDO— the Chief Data Officer. The CDO helps manage data as an important corporate asset. Here are the differences between the two:

Chief Analytics Officer	Chief Data Officer
• Business-centric role	• IT Centric Role
• Makes money out of data	• Legitimizes data
• Leverages data as a competitive advantage	• Keeps sanity of data through the IT systems
• Has an out-of-the-box thinking approach. Is agile, and has a clear understanding of the business value chain	• Follows a structured approach to implement IT principles and provides clear direction to maintain data integrity and sanctity
• Analytics processes owner	• Data Owner within the business
• Story Teller	• Data Protector

Team structure for delivering successful analytics projects

It is extremely important to have the analytics team structured right. While that concept is well understood, analytics is a holistic process, so different teams need to be equipped with different sets of capabilities and have different roles and responsibilities:

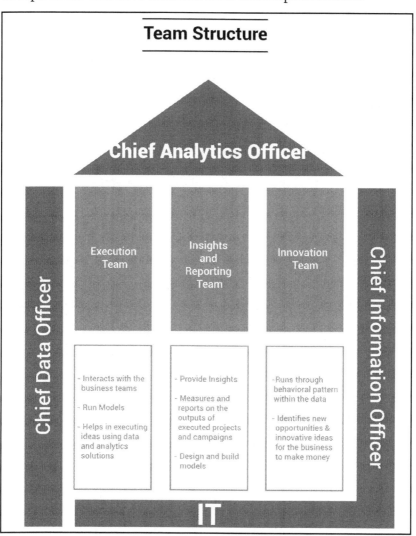

1. Execution Team

Role and Responsibilities:

The main objective of this team is to execute analytical models by taking data and providing for the design, build, testing and deployment of any analytical model which the business needs. This team is responsible from the very first step of data discovery all the way up to the modelling.

These are the people in whom the aspect of true comradeship is sought. They apply every model conjured in absolute conformity to business protocols and the guidelines set by the governing entity in order to produce valuable insight.

Skill Set:

- Innovators and quick thinkers
- Experienced to deal with tricky data
- Data management skills
- Data manipulation skills
- Statistical modelling skills

2. Insights Team

Roles and Responsibilities:

The insights team converts the output of the model into a report in simple English to be consumed by the business. They interpret the scores and outcomes of the statistical model and explain what it means for the business.

The insights team provide the analysis containing the recommendations which can solve the said business problem. The next step for the insight team is business integration, which as we discussed, incorporates working with the business team and management for these recommendations to be absorbed and implemented. The main task of the insight team is to build confidence with the business team so they can trust the outcome and help execute the findings.

Skills Set:

- Understanding of business and IT
- Statistical modelling skills
- Knowledge of data visualisation tools
- Strong presentation skills and visual art design skills
- Ability to convert the output of statistics into plain and simple English
- Storytelling skills
- Strong communication skills
- Passionate about business

3. Innovation team

Roles and Responsibilities:

This team is solely responsible for the innovation of new ideas and seeking out more exciting opportunities from the data. They recognise new patterns, see new behaviours and find out what these things might mean for the business. Their job is to consistently dive deep into the sea of data and find the hidden treasures.

Skills Set:

- PhD in statistics and related fields
- Advanced statistical modelling skills
- Curious about data
- Hacker mindset with problem-solving ability
- Innovators and out-of-the-box thinkers
- Understanding of the business and business processes

The three teams mentioned above are under the leadership of the Chief Analytics Officer. To be precise, the job of CAO of an organisation is to make money out of data. This person must have experience and expertise in both business and IT, and must have the ability to integrate his knowledge of the two segments.

Explanation of Business Process

Sophistication Levels in Business in the context of analytics:

The below picture aligns the business function with the analytics processes. To understand this, we need to understand how a business operates and makes decisions on a day-to-day basis.

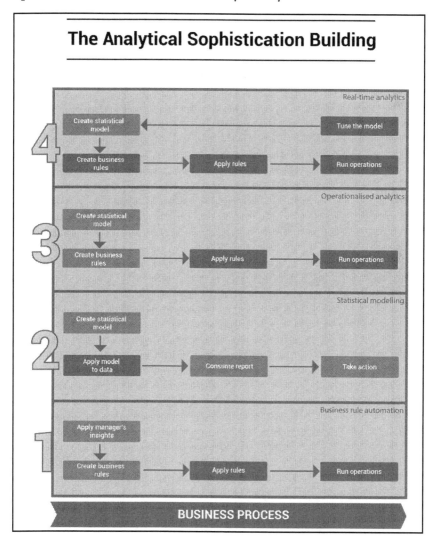

The baseline of any business remains the same at a fundamental level: a report is developed based upon your plan, which would probably focus on the feasibility of the plan and the steps or processes to be implemented. The report is consumed by the business owner/manager and an action is taken on the plan.

There are various floors of automation/sophistication of a business which can be present in any company. Let us understand each one by taking an example of a bread manufacturer supplying its products to different states of the country. The business manager, Miguel, gets a report each week on the sales performance of the bread. Imagine the bread sales are down in a region for a few weeks.

Now let's see how each level of sophistication reacts to the situation.

Level 1 – Business Rule Automation

This is the first and most basic level where the intent is to simply solve the problem that has been reported. Insights, experience and the instincts of the people controlling the business are used to modify the existing business plan or model and new business rules are formed. The rules are applied and the operations are being run.

In the bread situation: Miguel looks at the report and then makes decisions based on his instincts. Based on his own understanding of the business, and his experience, he decides to drop the price by 10 percent and continue supplying it in the market. This action has no concrete logic, as such. Rather, it is his instinct. He might decide to do trial and error on a new cost after reviewing the results of sales after the ten percent price reduction. Fundamentally speaking, he did analyse the market; but his analysis was based solely on experience and instincts.

Level 2. Statistical Modelling

On this level, statistical models are built offline and then learnings/insights are consumed by the business managers through reports to act.

Once the problem is identified, a statistical model is tested and built to understand the reasons behind the problem. The output of the statistical model is a set of insights and based on the insights a set of recommendations in the form of a report is presented. The report is consumed manually, and then the decision is to decide what action should be taken. The modelling work provides the insights and recommendations to the decision makers which helps them to make data-driven decisions and take action. As this is a one-off action, the next action requires another set of modelling and there is no integration or learning from the output.

Miguel invites an external agency, which performs statistical modelling to meet with him. As a result of the modelling exercise, they find multiple insights and recommend to Miguel that he only drop the price of bread in the region where the geo-economic status of the population is low and the income levels are within a particular range. The campaign would end after the demand is stabilised. However, the stability won't last forever, and the demand would go down again. The agency will have to be called again to do the modelling.

Level 3. Operationalising the Modelling

Statistical models are built offline and then model outputs are directly fed into the operations, allowing systems to take action for various scenarios.

In the third level of sophistication, once the problem is identified, modelling is done, the output of the modelling exercise is turned into business rules which are embedded into the operational systems. The actions are automated and run without any human interaction. Actions are automatically executed every time the rules are met. The only challenge arises when the model gets out of sync with the data behaviour, as that requires re-calibration of the model, usually in a few months. The modelling exercise has to be redone to create the model again before embedding it back into the system.

Miguel asks the external agency to create business rules using statistical analysis for the drop-in sales for bread. Once the rules are created, the agency hands them over to the IT team (in-house or outsourced) and the IT team embeds these changes in the system. The next drop-in demand is identified by the system and the suitable business rule is picked up which defines the alteration in the price of bread in the given specific areas. This reduces the time taken for the implementation of the business rule and automates the process.

Level 4. Real Time Analysis

Models recalibrate themselves in the operational environment using machine language based on the behavioural data and take action.

The real-time analysis is the last floor of sophistication where even the model is re-calibrated by itself once it is out of sync. In level three, the human intervention is vanished to an extent and the system continues to work on its own. However, once the data behaviour changes, the model would require re-calibration, after a certain period of time. The fourth level removes the need to recalibrate the model manually to change it.

The environment, in this case, provides the ability to alter models in real time using advanced analytics and machine learning so that the problem is solved before it happens. The feedback data is being consistently consumed to re-calibrate the models in an advanced cognitive environment.

In the case of our bread example, by making observations over the behaviour of market and customers, the drop-in demand is being predicted beforehand and models are being recalibrated to create modelling outputs which are consumed automatically to take business actions which are altering the business practices in a way that the predicted problem never becomes a reality in first place. There is little or no human intervention in this level of sophistication. Hence, the problem doesn't occur in reality. Miguel is consuming the reports only to see that everything is functioning smoothly.

Benefits of Analytics

What is the objective of a business? This question can solicit multiple answers depending on the ideologies and the strata of the individuals answering. While value creation or instituting a change or a revolution sound like idealistic answers, in the end, the bottom line of all businesses is to make more money. Call it capitalism or whatever term you prefer this is the 24-carat truth.

Bluntly put, any activity undertaken while the resources of the business are being utilized should result primarily in two things:

- Profit Increment – companies make more and more money
- Cost optimisation– reduce the costs incurred for various processes

Analytics, in the end, helps with the same two objectives mentioned above. The outcome of analytics, and the alterations it brings to business processes and policies, will ultimately lead to making more money for the organisation. One of the key elements of analytics is to define the objective of the business problem that needs to be solved.

Profit increment

For any organisation, incremental profit can be achieved by targeting the following objectives:

1. Increase in Cross Sell and Up Sell

Data from one product does not only improvises the sales aspects of that particular product but it also opens up new avenues for a whole bunch of sales channels for your other products. It tells you how much the customers need a supplementary or a complimentary offering of yours compared to what they're buying.

To explain this, further, we need to understand the propensity of any customer to buy:

xiv. Ability to identify customers who are likely to buy a particular product and then offer it to them with the product they were originally going to buy, when they are ready to buy it.

xv. Ability to identify customers who are ready for a new product or ready to upgrade to a new model.

It's all about offering the right product at the right time to the right customer at the right place.

Data opens up the customer to you, opens you up to the customer. That's how you are able to gain enough insight to pitch your diverse self to the suitor. In some situations, when the product really loses all future possibility of business, what do you do?

Example: The customer has a mobile phone. If they belong to a particular segment of the population amongst whom data service is very popular, yet they don't have a data service, you cross-sell a data service to them. On the other hand, when a new phone comes on the market, identify a target audience who is likely to upgrade based on their profile.

2. Acquiring New Customers and expanding into new markets

If there's one thing we know in the world of business, it's the pain we have to go through to get a new customer interested in our business. The gimmicks and tricks we have to pull off, the beg-borrow and stealing we have to do, the plead, pitch, present and promote scenario that we have to create. But with data analytics, it all becomes very simple.

Data provides us with pragmatic and logical mapping of each comprehensive portion of any target population. Unless we love everyone, we can't sell to anyone, and thus we need to know everyone in order to sell to everyone, even if we haven't sold to them earlier. Data provides us with that power. Intent data—to measure the likelihood of someone buying anything and predictive analytics—the market study of how products are going to behave with respect to various factors, are both tools at our disposal just waiting to be used. There's not one product that cannot be sold to everyone irrespective of their age, gender, demographic position; all that has to be done is modulate the product with respect to the new customer and that cannot be done without knowing in quantifiable terms, what a customer wants.

To put it simply, analytics can provide you the following to enable the acquisition of new customers:

i. The ability to understand your target segment of the market for the product

ii. The channels they are likely to be acquired through

iii. An understanding of the gap within your market

Example: Considering the fact that people holding credit cards are likely to fly, airlines are now collaborating with credit card companies while using them as a channel to launch new credit cards which provide added benefits if the customer uses a particular airline. This is helping the airline companies target a new customer segment and expand into a new market.

3. Improving Lead Management

With the hustle going on around us with tools like the salesforce, people might wonder sometimes if we need these tools at all. But when it comes to managing leads, everyone has this feeling of not being able to reach their full potential. With data analytics, the gap between expectations and the reality of lead management can be minimized. Not every lead is to be handled in the same way. This is determined by the trend of the particular type of lead, and many other factors. Unless the data to prove it is there, the lead is as good as dead.

Past losses cannot be turned around, and past wins cannot be left as legacies. But something can be done about both of them, which is possible by using the standardized data that is present at our discretion. With data, we know the statistics of turnaround time, time in queue and service rate, and thus we know how to build trust in the prospect by providing something different in our pursuit of them as a customer. Even if we don't convert them to an actual sale, at least we've taken that lead to the next level.

Lead management has two components:

a. Identifying New Leads

Analytics can help identify people who are in the market for a particular product /service by using internal and external data.

b. Lead Conversion

As soon as these leads are identified, a new predictive score is calculated which can be easily used to define the probability of the lead to convert. This technique can significantly enhance the qualified leads and, of course, enable better lead management and more efficient follow-up processes within the teams of sales and marketing—eventually accelerating the success and growth of sales.

Example: A real estate website where people advertise to sell their houses and potential buyers can check the options is highly popular. An insurance company ties up with this website and obtains hot leads. This is the lead identification part. Now, with the help of analytics, the insurance company predicts the score, which relates to the likelihood of the lead getting converted and designs a campaign accordingly.

4. Improving Salesforce Effectiveness

Smart people never put their soul into trivial matters of business, they allocate and they delegate, which needs to be done in an even smarter way to actually bear the sweet fruit of success. The resources that are put to use in sales, be it man or machine, must be optimized according to the business in order to provide reasonable results. And monetized evaluation of sales efforts is how the salesforce is optimized. Analytics helps in:

- Improving operational metrics of the salesforce
- Bringing in automation to accentuate the time value of money lost in sales pipeline
- Cultivation of smart systems that sell-map-innovate on their own to suit the audience

None of these can be a miracle to the workforce by itself, but it has to be injected into the business by the logic of real time data. Knowing where you're wrong and acknowledging it is the first step towards solving a problem. And statistics about your own sales characteristics is the only method that offers you this opportunity.

The salesforce can be segmented into top, average and poor performers and then it can be analysed what the top performers were doing right. The same can be implemented to other segments. Reasons behind key metrics, which are not being catered to, can be identified and fixed.

Example: The salesforce of a bank complains that the IT systems of the company are slow and they are not able to do as many meetings and hence the sales were down. The IT teams said everything was in order. After all the data was analysed, it was found that the sales were low not because of IT, but because the salesforce team was having way too many internal meetings and hence didn't have enough time left to meet external clients and close sales.

5. Retaining Valuable Customers

Retention is simply the art of innovation inspired by long-standing customer relationships. It involves formulating concepts to imbibe loyalty and convince the customer to remain with your company. In order to keep them, you must know what makes them tick, what bores them and how to pamper them. You need to know the technical, social and psychological effects of every business decision and every platform modulation that you offer is aimed at retaining customers. How can one do this without having something tangible that has charted the customer's response? The answer is, there is something tangible from which to extract these answers. The secret of customer satisfaction lies in some dark dungeon of taupe-coloured desks.

Extracting that information and using it is what analytics is all about. Typically, people will say, smart marketing can render the same effect. But smart people understand that marketing is just a part of customer retention. The real issue—the tangible thing that charts a customer's response—is a journey that winds through product development, the supply chain, post sales care, feedback, marketing and beyond. Analytics can get into the information stored in the dark dungeons of taupe-coloured desks. It can offer insight into the entire sales chain by dipping into all these fields at once with the synchronized aim of buttressing customer retention.

- Analytics can figure out the customers who are likely to leave.
- It can further understand their behaviour, and the reason they are leaving as well as help create a strategy to retain them.

Using analytics to determine which customers are likely to leave, and why, makes the business's marketing efforts much more targeted, rather than trying to use broad brush strokes in an attempt to retain every customer.

Example: A telecom company analyses the behaviour of the customers and predicts the customers who are about to switch to another company. Accordingly, they run a campaign to bring new offers to these clients to convince them to stay with the company.

6. Improvising promotional effectiveness

Effectiveness is an epitome of operational streamlining; it's as easy as it should be. Optimization of resources helps ensure the job is done correctly in the fewest possible iterations. How is it done? By taking notes of errors in workable data format. If the work and its quality can be expressed in terms of parameters and the same can be measured and worked upon - it can reduce rework, rejection and wastage; and didn't we describe the working format of Data analytics in this previous sentence? Only presentable figures and understandable analogy can quantify what the gap in improvisation and current state, so for the lack of any other better option, it's good to use this Analytical way or slip into oblivion by not trusting its credibility. After all how can data tell if my marshmallow is spongy or not? Oh wait! Maybe it can.

- Analytics can help identify the right offer for the promotion
- It can also help improve its effectiveness by providing a clear understanding of the target market
- It can further improve the promotion over a period of time based on responses to the promotion

Example: Placement of a billboard promoting a particular automobile brand was decided after applying analytics to help choose which highway in the city promised the maximum effectiveness.

7. Optimising pricing of a product

The pricing of a product is critical and can have an impact on customer behaviour as well as the profitability of a company. To understand the concept of pricing, demand, sales and profits, it is important to understand the cost journey of the product. There is a certain cost that the company incurs for any product or service being offered, which is basically the cost price. The company sells this product or service at the selling price. The difference between the two is simply the profit per unit. It is obvious that increasing the selling price might result in a customer purchasing a smaller quantity (considering that the customer has fixed purchasing capacity). In this case, the profit per unit is increased, but the number of units sold has decreased, reducing the overall profit (number of units sold multiplied by profit per unit). The cost has to be increased or decreased in such a way so as to increase the overall profit. Analytics help predict the increase and decrease in demand based on cost. It help identify the most optimum cost to produce the maximum overall profit.

Example: Bread is being sold at a retail store and the fluctuations in demand severely impact the profits. Analytics help establish a relationship between the fluctuating demand and the cost that must be established to ensure maximum possible profits.

8. Channel Expansion and Optimization

Data not only gives us a real-time view of current status, but it also helps us to manage the crests and troughs in the landscape of ever changing markets. Taking on a market means applying the art of exploiting multiple channels. Data analytics helps identify the feeders of various channels for communication, sales and purchasing; in all internal and external forms. It gives information on what's required for their sustainability and what clogs should be cleared from the channels. Expanding channels through efficient cross breeding needs to be done with care, or the entire system could be destroyed. Cross-channel marketing, integration of Point of Sale with Website and Online Channel data; Customer

/ Product Relationship Management with partner portal and sales compensation data are all the brainchild of the data-based revolution. Exhaustion, improvement, depletion and adulteration in any such parameter implicitly reflects in the qualitative analysis of all possible channels used by any business.

- Analytics can help understand the market needs to drive channel expansion
- Analytics also determines what offerings should be most relevant and can be most profitably driven through those channels

Example: A clothing company focused on offline retail stores explores the possibility of using online channels to drive better sales with the help of analytics. Analytics unveils insights about their customers' profiles to see that their core segment is youth attuned to mobile phones. Understanding this allowed them to shift from an offline and website-based business to a mobile app only business. The new strategies were devised in sync with this insight to attain success with the new channel.

9. Target New Market

Searching for new marketing frontiers is a bit like the Starship Enterprise heading into the deep recesses of space without knowing what strange new adventurers await them. This cannot be done without modelling, remodelling and testing business objectives in hostile conditions in order to understand how they work, and then making them failsafe.

- Analytics allows you to know about yourself and thus more about the market in which you're currently in.
- You're able to identify what may work and what might not in the new market.

Example: A retail company is highly successful in one city and now they want to expand into other cities. With the help of analytics, they can successfully figure out the demographics of the new market and the kind of priority products the company should launch. Also, a detailed competitor study can be done to know what has worked in the market and how they can design better campaigns to boost sales.

2. Cost Optimisation

In an organisation, there is a cost for every little thing one can imagine. From hiring new employees to managing the infrastructure that is enabling the business—everything costs something. And this slice of the cost is taken from the f profits that are being made. If the cost is less, the company can better enjoy the bigger profits. Cost optimisation of this slice is something analytics can help with.

a. Improvised efficiency and time reduction

Data coming from multiple sources within an organisation can help identify various inefficient processes and the reasons driving those inefficiencies. With the use of advanced analytics techniques, these inefficiencies can be easily identified and optimised to improve the processes, thus improving on time delivery.

Example: When data from a project is collated together and run through advanced analytics models, it can help identify the key block points in the projects and the drivers leading to the block points. If the drivers are taken care off, the blockages are reduced significantly. This helps in reducing delivery time for certain projects.

b. Streamline General, Administrative and Support costs

A business is constituted of multiple segments/departments, and these have a cost that the company needs to bear. At the same time, the departments also have a number of internal and external processes, like hiring new employees, developing new infrastructure, outsourcing services and vendor management. The cost for each of these processes can be reduced with the help of analytics. Consider a company with high attrition rates where new recruits are leaving quickly. Analytics can give the company insights into how this can be stopped, thereby helping the company reduce the cost of hiring.

c. Helps to stay updated

With the ever-changing market trends and availability of a plethora of options, it is quite predictable that consumers can change their mind easily. In this situation of instability, analytics will ensure certainty; it will help to have a better idea about the target audience. Analytics will also prompt companies to cope with the ever-changing needs of the consumers and minimize the chances of lagging behind. Keeping tabs on the changing market trends helps with creativity and bringing in new and possibly better ideas. This ultimately improves the flow of information, services and products.

We all know how rapidly changes are taking place in the industry. We have witnessed many incidences of start-ups taking over the industry giants. Analytics will guide you to deal with the unpredictability related to your business, and will help you craft your plans and products according to your clients' demands.

d. Better alternatives for making money

Analytics is not limited to modification or alteration of the existing product cycles or internal processes to achieve profit increments or cost optimization. Investing in analytics can open avenues which have been hiding out of plain sight. We will learn more in subsequent sections about finding new opportunities.

-10-

Success stories
Companies that have done it well

The importance of analytics and how it functions has been highlighted in a paramount fashion by now. But the question is: are companies actually making use of analytics? Or they still consider it an alien entity and shying away from it? Here are some of the facts that reflect how accepting companies and business have been toward analytics.

Very few companies believe that their organisation has access to the right data

Most of organisations focus on getting data, yet they think they do not have enough data, or the right data for analytics. They feel that they need more and more data that needs to be right to run in analytics. But, how much is more? In the process of getting more and more data, the organisations forget that they are not exploiting the goldmine of data they are already sitting on and thus, missing huge opportunities.

Most companies recognize that they will have to tap into external data sources

Internal data sources alone won't suffice. Hence, companies now recognize the need to tap into external data sources which can supplement their internal data. There can be various sources of this external data which is subjective to the nature of the business problem. Tapping external data is useful, but it has to be done on a case-by-case basis. There are a number of reasons why more and more businesses and data professionals are incorporating external data analytics into their decision-making processes. With the advent of social media and the availability of large amounts of data that is easily accessible highlights why now is the perfect time to go all in on external data.

Very few companies believe they are getting the Return on Investment from analytics

As most of the companies do not apply the right approach and methodology and do not have the right people, they are not able to get a good return on their investment from analytics. Actually, they blame analytics as a function itself, and say that analytics does not give any returns. However, they fail to implement analytics appropriately and are not able to understand what to expect from analytics and how to get the most out of the analytics processes. Only a few companies have reaped the benefits of analytics. The reality, is that the analytics function, if implemented correctly, is always a profit centre as it can pay for itself.

Very few companies use Predictive Analytics to run business

Predictive analysis is used to analyse the historical and current data to make predictions in a wide variety of areas. Though it has been around for a long time, it is now becoming popular because of better access to technology, complimented by stern economic conditions where it is critical to have competitive advantages.

Such predictive models can cater to a wide number of objectives, yet still, predictive models cannot be the driving force of analytics. The driving force has to remain the business problem, or perhaps, finding out the right business problem and framing it.

Very few companies have hired a Chief Analytics Officer (CAO)

The job of a Chief Analytics Officer is to make money out of data and discover new and innovative ways to do it. However, companies often not only underestimate the importance of a CAO, but they also misunderstand the role. Companies usually confuse it with a Chief Data Officer whose job is to get the right data and ensure consistent supplies and sources for the data they need. A lot of companies appoint a CDO and expect him to deliver what a CAO should, and worse than that, the appointed officer is settled in with the IT department.

However, the attitude of the company and its ability to remain open to ideas paves the way for analytics to change the way they function.

There are basically three situations in a business:

1. The Known Knowns: Things We know, We Know

These are the things that a company knows they know. For this, the company has the right data, right insights and the traditional analytical techniques are able to exploit these for good. Companies find confidence in this because of a simple fact—it is in line with their own knowledge and scope of imagination and hence provides a certain level of comfort. Usually, business intelligence platforms help to explain using reports and slicing/dicing of data.

2. The Known- Unknowns: Things We know, We Don't Know

These are the aspects that the company knows they don't know. They might have the data but not the right method or technique to use it. This creates a possibility for a core advanced analytics team to be invited in so that the unknown can be known.

3. The Unknown-Unknowns: Things We Don't know, We Don't Know

These are the aspects which a company doesn't know, nor do they have a realization that they don't know it. It implies that they don't even know what they are trying to find. As I have always said—analytics is not about finding the right answer. It is all about asking the right questions. The biggest problem with companies is that they don't know the right question—which is the classic case of unknown-unknowns. This is the most difficult territory, and this is where companies are found to be rigid. However, at the same time, these are the situations where jaw-dropping revelations come to light and things which were never even imagined, are achieved. This is all about pattern recognition and identifying hidden patterns within the data.

Companies that have successfully utilised analytics to get benefits

The way analytics functions is both complex and simple depending on the perspective of the onlooker. Analytics has various levels of sophistication in which it functions, and a business might still be on the journey to inward layers of analytics from the outward layers which are more broad and basic. Here are few examples of companies and their respective levels of sophistication in regards to their use of analytics, and how they are extracting benefits from this use:

1. Gathering data from untapped sources - Kraft Foods

As we discussed before, keeping people at the heart of analytics is important—and that's exactly what Kraft Foods did. The analytics on social media data was indeed, dazzling. They argued that social media offers them a huge set of data—bigger than anything else, and the best part about it is the fact that social media data is being refreshed regularly on its own. People talking about their breakfast on social media—both good and bad—is a form of consumer reaction to the product which can be used to decide the alteration in the product or the related attributes like packaging, marketing, distribution and more.

Why does it make more sense? Traditionally speaking, you ask a question to individuals or a focus group to get the data. Using this method implies you are simply listening to a conversation. This gives them an idea of what the end user is thinking and perhaps wishing for. Be it analysing flavour trends, usage trends or simply understanding if they liked the small gift you gave them with the packet—data through social media can give you all of it.

Thus, applying analytics on social media data provides a larger and more verified data with accounts of susceptibility of the consumer demand and their perception not only in terms of their specific opinion about one thing, but also their general opinion about a wholesome concept. Kraft Foods mapped ethnography charts of the population and used social media keyword tracking in order to seek information about complementary and supplementary products that Kraft Foods produced for those products, which were the talk of the town, but were not being produced by Kraft Foods or any of the subsidiaries.

2. Improving functional activities through analytics – Janssen Pharmaceuticals

Janssen Pharmaceuticals used to follow the same traditional method of marketing that every other company was doing. The idea was simple: Find the physicians who are prescribing the drugs that they are manufacturing and then oblige these physicians in a way that they prescribe the company's manufactured drugs. External agencies were being hired to find a list of such physicians whom the sales representatives can go to and approach. This costs the company extra. These lists would clearly highlight 80 percent of top physicians who could fit the criteria and the sales team will decide whom to visit first and then they would hand out the samples, a few complimentary gifts, event invitations and whatever else had been planned by the company to make them happy.

This process had been working for Janssen Pharmaceuticals and their partners for the past many years. So, when the in-house marketing analytics team said that no outside firm had to be sought to generate such generic data about the right physicians to approach, the managers and Chief Information Officers were dumbfounded. So much data was retrieved and made useful by the data analytics team for Janssen, that three months after presenting and beginning to work on this idea, they had saved the company almost 1.5 million U.S. dollars. Money that would have been wasted on paying an outsourced firm to gather intel when the internal analytic teams could get the data themselves.

With the help of analytics, the company developed a complex propensity scoring model. The model could tell them about the behaviour of doctors, and if they would prescribe a particular medication only if they had samples or vouchers, or if they would like to know more about the drug through an expert. With the help of these insights, the company could reduce the list of physicians to be approached by half, making their methods more efficient. They were able to save time by knowing exactly what the doctor wanted from them, and save money by reducing their salesforce.

In the subsequent fiscal years, Janssen was able to reduce the redundant marketing practices and expenditures by a factor of 10. They were able to map the customer reviews and ROI proximity while approaching various doctors and prescribers based on the local customer reviews of their clinics and practice history. They were able to map the marketing and strategic initiation of products in various regions by using information from the health diagnostics and check-up firms, which provided an insight into mobilizing concerns of people in a closed society regarding any particular medical ailment.

Getting direct data on customer reviews about their medicines, mapping genetic influences of their globally manufactured medicines on various ethnicities and mobilization of local sales were all possible by mapping various data sets collected periodically from various channels of services, including the conventional focus groups.

Project Data Sphere, a cloud-based data sharing initiative, is also a part of Janssen's data analytics marvels. This project allows for various contributors, and even competitors in the same market, to collaborate and produce various forms of data sets collected over time from various channels like supply chain observations, social media channels, government reports, biological datasets, surveys and campaign outcomes on a single cloud-based database. Accessible to all and restricted by none, all this cross-functional data, when laid at the disposal of analytics giants is revolutionized in unprecedented ways to formulate new medicines, create artificial intelligence models for simulations, develop targeted campaigns and build collaborative initiatives to develop the overall industry. To date, many partners, subsidiaries and competitors like Astra Zeneca, Bayer Celgene Sanofi, etc., are avid participants of this Janssen Project.

Having just the data is never enough. But having ways to harness the benefit that every data set can provide is essential. Strategic logging and maintenance of data is a great asset for any organisation, and Janssen's example clearly exhibits this skill. We'll also get to know that simple applications of data evaluations, almost in their most basic formats are so useful sometimes that they supersede the necessity of any big data management.

3. Using analytics to improve distinct capability – Coca-Cola

Coca-Cola is a brand that needs no introduction. The advertisement campaigns of this brand have been fresh, catchy, innovating and pleasing. As expected, the company is just as innovative when it comes to analytics, as well. Cola-Cola installed a drink dispenser called Freestyle, which could mix 30 different flavours of soda, tea, flavoured water and more, to make more than 100 new flavours. The consumption of the new drinks resulted in unique behavioural patterns. The consumption trends are being noted since the machine sends data to the servers every single night.

The data will be used for operational activities (automatically scheduling refills, stopping distribution if there's a product recall of a particular cartridge, etc.) and for analytics. This will assess how new drinks are doing in the market, identifying differences in regional tastes, and helping fast-food outlets decide which drinks to serve. It's like creating data while catering to the needs of the consumer and satisfying the higher purpose of providing the consumer with the best.

Coca-Cola, like any other beverage company, had huge problems with the introduction of sugar for people living in the U.S.A. and the Soda Tax in Mexico; but as some great souls have said, 'a problem in itself is an opportunity in disguise'. What Coca-Cola did was use their data analytics team to track the legislative proceedings and also to generate data of biological mapping for sugar decay cycles in their soft drinks to identify the mobilisation of the public with respect to their response towards the new law. The new data consumption and the regional response data gathered from the biological mapping compared with the report generated for measurement of carbonate and glucose compounds in their products led them to carefully optimise and plan their way. Now they were able to develop the product and at the same time pacify the legislature, as well, and all of that by just making efficient use of data.

With Coca-Cola, the usage of data analytics has not just been limited to mapping customer reviews, it has also been used to design the volume and sales mapping from bottlers all around the world. In an amazing application of its internal data analytics, they have been able to perform more forward-looking analytics than backward-looking analytics which are the tools of checks and balances made for actions of the past. For identifying the most economic raw material acquisition method and managing the export economies of cross-country brands of Coca-Cola, the hypotonic and particulate content of the fruit based drinks has also been regularly mapped by various teams. It's like the same brand of Minute Maid bottled in Nagpur has a different composition altogether from that produced in Philadelphia. Thus, identifying the acceptance of regional beverages when exported to other countries was determined by campaign management of social media reviews with respect to ethnic polling.

In this way, selective marketing and export economies have been another feather in the cap for the data analytics team for Coca-Cola all around the world. Coca-Cola is hoping to use its new analytic power to speed up and improve test marketing processes with the ability to try out new flavours with almost real-time feedback. That information can then be quickly shared throughout their worldwide distribution channels.

4. Back to the basics with Data Analytics: Lessons in efficient Visualizations of data – Procter and Gamble

Public opinion about beauty supplements, skin care products and other consumer products is always a volatile concept. Many companies succumbing to the nature of market have always kept profound catalogues of data, but only a few of them have been able to use those catalogues in sensible ways. Procter and Gamble was a company burdened with the data of results collected from rigorous marketing campaigns. They simply went back and followed the rules of efficient data visualisation in order to bring out the best in the industry practices. Having processed data without any way to explain it, move it, record or replicate it in order to extract insights and work on conclusions was the problem Procter &Gamble was facing. Then they created an artificial intelligence-based model of data analytics called Control Tower to monitor the market alternate for inbound, outbound raw materials along with their movement cost which was monitored in real time across various sites. With such data being displayed in real time to the managers of global data centres, continuous and updated strategic protocols were being made which supported the total supply chain management.

The cloud analytics tool for global marketing was also formulated in order to keep a tab on data warehousing and analytics. Such data was reflected in the findings of simulated 'Touchpoint' readings from regional sales channels. Data that is generated is stored on cloud platforms for managers around the world to access. Multiple search data is merged and in compatible formats is ready for user-suited interpretations.

To promote ready usage of data analytics results, all this company had to do was make the data visible enough to every one of its workers in order to ensure that many practices were formulated all around at global sites. One such practice was to set up handheld equipment at a production line to download data on inventory and supply (internal as well as external), thereby monitoring plant analytics from offsite locations. Another search method was also applied for increasing the accountability of manager and worker with respect to customer reviews on a daily basis. Setting up of real time phone lines for process managers to listen to the customer reviews regularly was a very great move in order to charter the data gathered from Teradata Marketing Analytics in the right way with respect to fresh opinions from the user.

Their in-house data crunching team was already heavily experienced and proficient enough to analyse all the data gathered, but the data just wound up in files or reports and was never put to good use because nobody knew how to properly visualise how the data could be used. The simple method of making data available to business stakeholders and project managers after gathering it from various channels to project the findings in the right direction was what made this Consumer Products firm the leading producer of its time.

5. Tesco Analytics – No stone left unturned and no data left uncrunched

The amount of data that everyday stores can generate in order to identify the consumer trends and interests is incomparable. Tesco, like any other utility store franchise, was quick to identify this idea and thus it left literally no stone unturned in order to make use of all the insights that it could take in from even the lollypop licking toddler that visited its stores.

Identifying the latest trends in online shopping, the clothing and lifestyle wing of Tesco found that the window of sales opportunity was lost in their brick and mortar stores due to limited options and personalization in comparison to the plethora of products their customers could buy online; they were desperate to solve this nexus. In running quick simulations with their data sets, the analysis indicated that when people were trying to buy in a physical store, they may be overwhelmed with the number of choices they have, but while shopping online, they are presented with a formulated approach so they can immediately eliminate irrelevant choices. But the meagre sensation of being presented with uncountable options is what allures the buyers these days and thus they introduced in-store kiosks so their customers can order things online. If a customer was unable to find the correct size or colour or a particular print, they could just go to one of the in-store kiosks and scroll through the Tesco Collection and order that product online and have it delivered to them at the store for pick-up. This brought the Tesco Online Store into competition with regional online stores and has done very well for the lifestyle section of the company.

Their club cards and loyalty analytics successfully led them to build a database of 38 million registered users, with almost 16 million active users. This not only provides them with a huge consumer base, but also provides them valuable insights with respect to buying patterns and inventory management; which stocks to hold and which stocks to dump, etc. Weather mapping and predictive analytics of its effects on purchasing patterns of various age groups has led them to develop strategies for maintaining most optimised stocks of Off-The-Barn products such as groceries, milk supplements, natural drinks and other very fast moving natural consumables.

Tesco Connect, which is another programme that has been run by the Tesco analytics team, is another example which helps store managers keep a tab on those items which, according to their customer dynamics and regional specifications, should be kept in stores to optimise sales and reduce wastage.

In fact, when we talk about the gist of being optimised and efficient, Tesco went a step ahead. To ensure sustainable workspace usage, they started to work on mapping their carbon footprints across stores in collaboration with a big software company. But eventually, data revealed, in what was just initiated to monitor the footprint, some awesome statistics on how the usage of electricity in all the stores across Europe could be streamlined in order to save on electricity bills in all stores of the nation. Once they discovered this angle of this project, the original idea of mapping carbon footprints was left for later and they put all their emphasis on optimising the usage of the refrigerators in stores. A whopping $25 million was saved each year from only the British Territory after the results of these modelling and strategies were implemented.

After analysing the effects, it could produce in customer experience and store schematics, Tesco gave its daily, essential, and pivotal actions at both macro organisational levels and micro levels like stores and warehouses to the business of data analytics. Using data analytics in ways like artificial intelligence models to automated store operations to usage of Regression Models for measuring shifting trends in any daily consumer items, Tesco soon became the world's fourth largest retail store brand.

6. Netflix: The House of Analytics –Where actions sans data are unimaginable

Netflix, the online entertainment giant which now has 70 million users worldwide, based all its business tactics on data analytics. The success of all its popular content is owed to the teams at its data centres, which generate heaps of data from each user activity registered on servers.

Netflix uses the very specific art of disruption mingled with close-circuit tappings of user activity while people are watching any of its content. Every pause and fast forward, scrolling patterns as users determine what they want to watch or pass on, social media mentions about Netflix, their customers' age and the algorithms generated to map their psychological interest points are all being constantly recorded at Netflix data Centres.

The formulation of onboarding algorithms which record the personal profile of the user along with the suggestions that he/she makes to fellow users while joining Netflix (which is an essential part of the initiation) have generated good sums of personalised data logs for each user based on their tastes and interests which helps Netflix push specific suggestions to specific people on their charts.

The touchpoint analytics formulated by their people concentrates specifically on how the data is gathered, and especially, which data is relevant in order to provide realistic usable information.

This would not only lead to monetary profits, but also ensure that the system itself learns from the data it receives, thereby creating a base for insights into future actions the company should take. They discard the data which does not provide them with any usable information or any information that does not hold any future value.

Netflix formulated a list of 300 different application tests that each content waiting to be published must pass through (it even has a test for the usage of colour schemes in content frames, which influence the stress on the eyes of users) in order to go live.

Netflix analytics is able to modulate not only the marketing and data design parts of their product, but also the technical aspects of the delivery framework and even the website appearance itself is susceptible to what is acceptable in various regions., They can map which people in the world are more tolerant for video buffering and who is not, and then compare the infrastructural compatibility that the region offers. In other words, they are able to modulate the technical aspects of their delivery to optimise their expenditures by providing only what a user will tolerate in some cases, but then providing what users demand, in other cases. Similarly, they work on various other aspects such as bit rate, pixelation, etc.

The mirroring data generated from re-watches and re-views that occur all over the world are used to determine strategic actions such as server setups, delivery channels, pricing, advertisements, discounts, etc. Each time signals bounce off any Netflix server, a policy parameter directly affecting the customer is tweaked. Therefore, each user behaviour changes or shapes the behaviour of Netflix in ways that can't be imagined.

7. Policy and workplace modulation based on analytics: The curious case of Google

Google uses data analytics for itself only for internal optimization for policy makeovers to manage resources rather than for business or marketing purposes.

The best application Google has so far done with its data analytic skills is the revamping of its HR management policies based on revelations made by some critical datasets. They have been able to expurgate the recruitment process of new candidates. How they did that was quite technical: they found the factors that influenced the competency and value of the onboarding processes. They look at things like the 'time value of the interview stages', mental profiling of candidates and measuring the increase in the skill level of recruits vs. data of fresh recruits leaving within one year to formulate onboarding policies, etc.

Google has a separate department for such analytical profilings and jobs which they personally like to call the People Operations department. They've done work on developing the matrix models for mapping employee life cycles, developed algorithms for the review of job applications to look for any missed candidates who by some freak chance had been left out (however, the datasets of Google itself indicate that they have a miss rate of as low as 1.4%). They further optimized 'leave and vacation' economies along various business sites based on the statistical study of medical competence, social behaviour and ethical and regional obligations based on society and religion. All this, when reported in 2013, lead to an annual savings of nearly 150 working hours per year for every new recruit.

Examples of initiatives based on data analytics can be given for Google which have been used to bring in necessary business standardization at the workplace, such as Project Oxygen, which was developed for figuring out the most important basic aspects of office ethics and behaviours essential to managers for the formal aggrandizement of their subordinates. Project Janus was the artificial intelligence program made to assess the missed candidates from the interviews as mentioned earlier here. Pi Lab was like an indigenous 'Kobayashi Maru' for Google employees, a situation simulator for predictive analysis and training of all employees including managers and leaders. All of them were formulated and setup after careful analysis of data observed in employee performances, problem-solving approaches, participation in community services and events, salary increments, leaves, etc.

Google works industriously on data, not only for human resource management, but also for intangible resource optimization, and in time, it has reaped good fortunes for the company. Patent IQ, was a program Google used for strategic planning of its patent filing calendar throughout the year. With the patent cases moving through courts in their own ways, with legislatures and amendments coming in and going out, with officials coming in going out, Google decided to analyse their past filing experiences. They looked at filling their backlog timings, dismissals, stalling costs, and which patents should be filed at which point of the year under which court and with how many other such filings, all so that they could discover the most optimized outcomes with the most minimum expenditures.

Google, in an altogether different sense, has utilized analytics along a different path in order to bring strict profitability to the organisation by the usage of data.

-11-

Summary

Analytics is a powerful friend if you know it well. But, sometimes even the best of friends proves to be ineffectual if not handled carefully. This is my story of using and sometimes overusing my best friend – Analytics.

In the past chapters of this book, I narrated my experience of working on the five major projects I worked on during my career. All five projects have different key messages about analytics. These messages must be understood and practiced to be able to make money out of data.

Data and analytics are like twin brothers: To understand one, the other must be studied and understood. This is what I aspire to do with this book. By narrating my personal experiences, I hope to make the subjects of data and analytics a little more relatable and exciting.

This book aims to be a guiding point for different organisations and individuals who want to understand the power of data and analytics. If understood and implemented well, analytics can make millions of dollars for you as well. All you need to do is embrace the power of data and equip it with creativity, innovation and the correct business knowledge.

I have also busted some myths around analytics and given real life examples on how analytics can be used to discover what has been hiding, and how this discovery can make millions of dollars for a company.

Every organisation wants to increase its sales and revenues, but analytics goes way beyond just helping increase profits. Analytics can help you understand your customers' behaviour better; find new customers and uncharted territories; improve your products and services; and a million other things just waiting to be discovered. Analytics has the power to transform big businesses, both in positive and negative ways.

I always say to my team members: companies which do not use data analytics are almost blind and deaf in their approach toward the future. In time, they will become obsolete and cease to exist. Interestingly, organisations are still reluctant to make a shift from a post-data to a data-driven world. But those organisations that do make the shift, are sure to profit from the transition.

Made in the USA
Middletown, DE
01 June 2017